ENDORSEMENTS

To know the heart of God better, we simply need to open up the Scriptures. Ginny and Andrew go straight to the source, diving into the stories of the Old Testament to help readers uncover who God was to His people long ago, in a worthwhile effort to better understand how He lives inside our stories today. The discovery of God is a lifelong pursuit, but *Transcending Mysteries* is a good place to start.

> Michael W. Smith
> Singer-songwriter

Transcending Mysteries puts flesh and bone on the God who seems as untouchable as the wind as we see Him in the pages of the Old Testament. But as I read this book, the lines between the Jesus we know and the God we can only ponder of come together in a powerful way. Ginny and Andrew have created a thoughtful journey, making the Old Testament approachable and relevant to our everyday lives. A fantastic Bible study for any age.

> Cindy Morgan
> Singer-songwriter and author of *Dance Me, Daddy* and *Barefoot on Barbed Wire*

I'm a longtime fan of Ginny's and Andrew's songwriting and the way they dream up music. I'm thrilled these two deeply creative friends have also taken their talents to the written word. You'll love their thoughtful approach to the Old Testament and the way they contend with the harder issues. *Transcending Mysteries* is an inviting work for those longing to study the Bible alongside compassionate and creative thinkers like Andrew and Ginny. You'll be led closer to the heart of Jesus—the One to whom the Old Testament points.

> Kelly Minter
> Songwriter and author of *Wh̶̶̶̶̶* ̶̶̶̶̶̶n̶
> and *Wherever The River Runs*

Andrew and Ginny have a unique gift of calling us all into the true beauty and mystery that is essential to becoming a true follower of Jesus. *Transcending Mysteries* is a gift to those of us who need to recapture His true wonder.

Chris Seay
President of Ecclesia Bible Society, pastor of Ecclesia Houston, and author of *A Place at the Table*, *The Gospel Reloaded*, and *The Gospel According to Jesus*

Ginny and Andrew deftly weave Scripture and personal stories to deliver a book that reveals the heart of the Eternal. It is a brave, heartfelt and generous work.

Ian Morgan Cron
Speaker and bestselling author of *Chasing Francis* and *Jesus, My Father, the CIA, and Me*

TRANSCENDING MYSTERIES

TRANSCENDING MYSTERIES

WHO IS GOD, AND WHAT DOES HE WANT FROM US?

ANDREW GREER & GINNY OWENS

THOMAS NELSON
Since 1798

NASHVILLE   MEXICO CITY   RIO DE JANEIRO

Published in Nashville, Tennessee by Thomas Nelson. Thomas Nelson is a trademark of HarperCollins Christian Publishing, Inc.

Published in association with J. David Huffman for MAE/brandWAVESLLC.

Page Design and Layout: Crosslin Creative

Thomas Nelson titles may be purchased in bulk for educational, business, fund-raising, or sales promotional use. For information, please e-mail SpecialMarkets@ThomasNelson.com.

Unless otherwise indicated, Scripture quotations are taken from The Voice™ translation. © 2012 Ecclesia Bible Society. Used by permission. All rights reserved.

Scripture quotations marked ESV are from THE ENGLISH STANDARD VERSION. © 2001 by Crossway Bibles, a division of Good News Publishers.

Scripture quotations marked NIV are from Holy Bible: New International Version®, NIV®. Copyright © 1973, 1978, 1984, 2011 by Biblica, Inc. Used by permission of Zondervan. All rights reserved worldwide. www.zondervan.com.

Scripture quotations marked NKJV are from The New King James Version. © 1982 by Thomas Nelson. Used by permission. All rights reserved.

Scripture quotations marked NLT are from Holy Bible, New Living Translation. © 1996, 2004, 2007, 2013 by Tyndale House Foundation. Used by permission of Tyndale House Publishers, Inc., Carol Stream, Illinois 60188. All rights reserved.

Scripture quotations marked TLB are from The Living Bible. © 1971. Used by permission of Tyndale House Publishers, Inc., Carol Stream, Illinois 60188. All rights reserved.

* Note: Italics in quotations from The Voice are used to "indicate words not directly tied to the dynamic translation of the original language" but that "bring out the nuance of the original, assist in completing ideas, and . . . provide readers with information that would have been obvious to the original audience" (The Voice, preface).

ISBN: 978-1-4016-8040-4

Printed in the United States of America

15 16 17 18 19 20 [RRD] 6 5 4 3 2 1

For those who, like us, still seek the Mystery.

CONTENTS

ACKNOWLEDGMENTS

More than a co-authorship, this book is the collaborative effort of many people whose walk with faith has breathed life into our own. They have helped us delve below the surface by allowing us to recount the personal details of their stories in an effort to help us tell our own stories as we chip away at the mystery of the story of God and us. We owe a great debt for these permissions.

We are equally indebted to our Thomas Nelson friends for steering the course. Thank you Frank Couch for giving legs to this project and helping it walk the extra mile. Our editor Maleah Bell has pored over every idea and word with thoughtful encouragement, replacing first-time author fears with confidence through prods of affirmation and words of friendship. We are grateful. Thank you Blake Aldridge, Amy Stambaugh, and Kathy Armistead for seeing this project as more than a release date. And to Ashley Linne for bringing us to the table.

Amid the piles of paperwork that substantiate a book deal, our literary agent David Huffman navigated through legal jargon so we could focus on the heart of the matter, of which he also lent his personal investment.

Our oceanside cohort Bob Lackey provided beautiful views and even more beautiful friendship.

And to our openhearted families who invited us to the table of conversation in the first place—we love you most of all.

PREFACE

"'Hope' is the thing with feathers—
That perches in the soul—
And sings the tune without the words—
And never stops—at all—"

—Emily Dickinson

We fell in love with Jesus. Then we had to decide what to do with God.

As the most definitive written revelation of who God is, Scripture has always been vital in our stories of faith. The Old Testament has proved especially tough for those of us who have been persuaded by the gracious gospel of Jesus but also desire to surrender to a God we don't fully comprehend. We adore the Son of God. But what about God the Father?

As thinking disciples, for better or for worse, we are in this quandary with you.

Growing up in the evangelical South, we often encountered polarizing—and sometimes paralyzing—ideas and theologies. Legalism was tempered and ultimately trumped by no-strings-attached grace. Doctrines of despair were countered by creeds of deep surrender. When Sunday school answers strengthened rather than quelled our doubts, our hearts remained open.

Week after week, Wednesday after Wednesday, we showed up to discover, discern, and, in the end, worship. Why? Perhaps it was hope.

Whether our problems were out in the open or tucked inside the subtler context of private indiscretions, we knew that all was not right with the world. We knew that all was not right within our hearts. And in our most vulnerable moments, in those very human communities of faith, our hearts were cultivated to seek and know God, the Eternal—Jesus.

Many of our friends were raised in the paralysis of religious legalism. However, the two of us grew up being encouraged to have honest discussions, receiving extra measures of grace along the way. This dialogue is for both parties. In these pages, we want to discover, not dictate, God. And we want Old Testament scripture to be the invitation.

Did you just say, "Hold the phone"? We realize this is not a popular route. The Old Testament induces a corporate flinch in generations of disciples. Many of us have been hurt and manipulated by a toxic use of Scripture which shamed us away from God. At best, we have had to distance ourselves from the Old Testament Jehovah in order to surrender our hearts to the New Testament Messiah. However, we believe that all of Scripture, when paired with our personal experiences, is important in discovering how He works through us, how He moves in us, and what He wants from us.

We hope together we can move past seeing Scripture merely as a tool of corporate control or an out-of-context resource for America's latest prosperity preacher. Instead, we want to open the book that has been used to curb the mystery and silence the questions of spiritual seekers worldwide, to ask the heartfelt question: is the God of the Old Testament the same God we relate to and worship today? As we question and articulate what stumps us most, we hope to perpetuate faith through surrender to the mysterious Yahweh, whose reverent name in Jewish culture alludes to God's infinite "I AM" character that is continually being uncovered throughout our experience.

We attempt all of this with great humility, fully assuming responsibility for the limits of our words. Who are we to opine on the character of God? As Madeline L'Engle expressed in her book *Walking on*

Water: Reflections on Faith and Art, "If we are qualified, we tend to think that we have done the job ourselves. If we are forced to accept our evident lack of qualification, then there's no danger that we will confuse God's work with our own, or God's glory with our own."[1]

We attempt all of this with great hope.

So shall we discover together? Perhaps Scripture was always designed for this dialogue, so that the Spirit of God who so mysteriously roams over and through all created things would have an open channel to not just reveal Himself to us, but to live among us.

—Ginny and Andrew
April 2014

CHAPTER 1

MIDNIGHT OF THESE THINGS

"In our darker hours / We pray for eyes to see / In the midnight of these things . . ."

—Andrew Greer, "Midnight of These Things"

"Every question led to more questions, but they also led to more faith."

—John Ortberg, *Faith and Doubt*[1]

"Hope is a function of struggle."

—Brene Brown, *Daring Greatly*[2]

Andrew: I am the youngest of three boys. I asked my mom if she ever wished one of us had been a girl. She diplomatically replied, "No. Boys are easy." Fair enough. Watching my oldest brother chart his life's path always looked easy. Decisive, rational, and organizationally bent, Trey is a natural leader. He graduated from college, got married, bought a house, and had children—in that order. And when discussing the gray areas of life, Trey is often ready with a decidedly black-and-white solution. But his seemingly obstinate opinion is merely a catalyst for igniting meaningful debate. And I've personally observed his deep faith in action as he and his family's experiences have been muddied with not-so-soluble circumstances.

In July 2010, at age thirty-two, Stephanie, my brother's wife of eleven years, was diagnosed with breast cancer. Home research, doctor visits, and analyzing treatment options followed. Because of her family's harried history with the disease, the diagnosis was even more serious. Every precaution was taken. With three girls under the age of five—their youngest only four months old—Stephanie, with the support of Trey and the girls, was now fighting cancer.

My sister-in-law's surgery recoveries required her to abstain from lifting any substantial weight for several weeks. Simple tasks like changing Lily's diaper, consoling Carley after a tumble, or lifting Avery into her car seat were now impossible. On two different occasions, Trey and Stephanie invited me to visit Texas to help my sister-in-law with the toddling trio. And though I was a twenty-seven-year-old bachelor and touring musician with poorly refined skills in braiding hair, setting up a tea, and being sensitive, I gladly accepted the opportunity to supply the roles of preschool shuttle, cul-de-sac campsite tent builder, and Sonic "Happy Hour" chauffeur—where our confused hearts remembered that sometimes comfort is simply one slush away.

Late one night after Stephanie and the girls were in bed, Trey and I jumped in his Ford pickup for a drive. It was the first time since her diagnosis that we had some time alone. Growing up sons of a therapist, we learned early how to "throw up" our emotions, which is actually more restorative than it sounds. Tough questions were a part of our family's everyday conversations. So I opened our car-ride chat with a simple question: "How are y'all *really* doing?"

Trey explained to me that cancer was the hardest thing he and Stephanie had experienced together or individually. Though neither of their histories is without trauma, when they received the malignant news from Stephanie's doctor, Trey said that they felt they had two distinct options: they could distance themselves from God and use every human resource available to control the outcome and heal Stephanie, or they could press in to God.

"Andrew," he said, "we're pressing hard."

SURRENDER: FEAR AND FAST

READ 2 CHRONICLES 20:1–12.

After Jehoshaphat had solidified his throne by fortifying the nation and appointing regional judges, the Moabites, Ammonites, and some Meunites decided to attack him. ²Jehoshaphat heard about their plans.

Messengers: A huge army is *quickly* approaching *Jerusalem*. They are coming from Edom beyond the *Dead* Sea, but they have already reached Hazazon-tamar (that is Engedi *on the shore of the Dead Sea, about two days southwest of Jerusalem*).

³Jehoshaphat was afraid, so he sought the Eternal and required all Judah's citizens to fast. ⁴⁻⁵Everyone gathered together in Jerusalem from cities all over Judah to seek help from the Eternal. Jehoshaphat joined the assembly in the newly restored court at the Eternal's house and ⁶prayed before the people.

Jehoshaphat: O Eternal One, the True God of our ancestors, You are the True God in the heavens and the ruler over all the kingdoms and nations! You are so strong that none can survive when they oppose You. ⁷O our True God, You *demonstrated that power when You* exiled inhabitants of this land for Your people, Israel, and gave it to Your friend Abraham's children forever. *Please demonstrate it again, now, as we are attacked.* ⁸We have lived here and built a sacred house honoring Your reputation. *Now we will remind You of Solomon's words:* ⁹"If we encounter disaster *or disease* from wars, judgment, pestilence, or famine, then we will come to this house where You are and where your reputation is honored and beg for Your help. You will hear our cries and rescue us."

[10]Now *is the time to ask for Your help.* Men from Ammon, Moab, and Mount Seir (*the region in Edom* which You stopped Israel from destroying when they left Egypt) [11]are rewarding *our ancestors' mercy* by coming to steal our inheritance, which is Your land and which You gave to us. [12]Our True God, won't You judge them? We can do nothing to stop this huge army from attacking us; we don't know what to do, so we are asking for Your help.

FEAR

Andrew: Before we hear God's answer to King Jehoshaphat's collective cry for Judah, let's give Jehoshaphat's kingdom career some context to help us better research his interaction with God in 2 Chronicles 20.

Scripture compares King Jehoshaphat's leadership of Judah to David's exemplary spiritual reign of Israel less than a century earlier (2 Chron. 17:3–4). Instead of being persuaded by the people's repeated periods of pagan practices—often motivated by fickle emotions and an impatient need for instant gratification (sounds like my justification for my own unhealthy practices, also known as sin)—Jehoshaphat sought guidance from the Eternal, the True God. As a result of the authenticity of his Spirit-convicted leadership, he enjoyed good relations domestically and internationally, and Judah became a strong economic and military might in the Middle East (2 Chron. 17:5–19).

So Jehoshaphat's God-honoring response to the news of the attack against Judah is not surprising. But he is still human. And surrender is always a

> **Jehoshaphat's doubts are human. His questions are fair. His search for clarity from God in an unexplainable scenario is simply honest.**

process. Scripture says, "Alarmed, Jehoshaphat resolved to inquire of the LORD, and he proclaimed a fast for all Judah" (2 Chron. 20:3 NIV). Other translations describe him as having "feared" (NKJV) and being "terrified" (NLT). His first reaction is gut-driven. In the face of unpredictable danger, Jehoshaphat, a king, is visibly afraid.

When my brother and his wife first received Stephanie's devastating cancer diagnosis, they responded humanly: shock, fear, and sorrow. Before tackling the logistics of treatments, doctors, hospitals, insurance, and family, they grieved over the results with questions for the Eternal. *Why us? Why now? What next?*

In fear's segue to surrender, Jehoshaphat also questions God. And why shouldn't he? Judah is a God-focused nation ("We have . . . built a sacred house honoring Your reputation" [v. 8]) whose forefathers extended mercy to the very people who are now planning to pillage Judah ("Men from Ammon, Moab, and Mount Seir . . . are rewarding *our ancestors' mercy* by coming to steal our inheritance, which is Your land and which You gave to us. Our True God, won't You judge them?" [vv. 10–12]). Jehoshaphat's doubts are human. His questions are fair. His search for clarity from God in an unexplainable scenario is simply honest.

Ginny: Jehoshaphat is alarmed by the threat of attack. And his questioning is justified. But despite their unknowable circumstances, many translations recount how he and his people "seek the LORD." "Then Jehoshaphat was afraid and set his face to seek the LORD. . . . And Judah assembled to seek help from the LORD" (2 Chronicles 20:3–4 ESV).

The phrase "seek the Lord" is a familiar one in church circles. We find it often in Scripture, sing it in hymns, and even use it in conversations, particularly about discerning God's will. However, "seek" is not a word that we often use on its own. When I think how

Jehoshaphat and Judah were quick to seek the Lord after receiving the terrifying news of impending attack, I stop to ponder what "seek" actually means.

My iPhone dictionary app defines *seek* as "to try to get or reach" or "to try to locate or discover." But if we cannot physically reach or locate God, what does it mean for us to seek Him?

After proclaiming a fast throughout Judah, Jehoshaphat stands in the temple courts before his subjects and prays. He doesn't begin this public supplication by laying before God the trouble at hand. Instead, he first acknowledges God's greatness. He prays, "O LORD, God of our ancestors, you alone are the God who is in heaven. You are ruler of all the kingdoms of the earth. You are powerful and mighty; no one can stand against you!" (2 Chron. 20:6 NLT).

In my own prayer life, I've been learning that seeking the Lord begins by acknowledging who He is. By recognizing Him as God before I get to my "please help" list, my anxiety quickly diminishes. My perspective changes from one in which I am in control and responsible for my own destiny to one where the Lord is in complete control of everything.

As Jehoshaphat asks God his questions and pleads for help, he also remembers the Eternal's history of faithfulness to the Jews for generations. "O our God, did you not drive out those who lived in this land when your people arrived? And did you not give this land forever to the descendants of your friend Abraham? Your people settled here and built this Temple to honor your name. They said, 'Whenever we are faced with any calamity such as war, plague, or

> **If we cannot physically reach or locate God, what does it mean for us to seek Him?**

famine, we can come to stand in your presence before this Temple where your name is honored. We can cry out to you to save us, and you will hear us and rescue us'" (2 Chron. 20:7–9 NLT).

I have to wonder if Jehoshaphat's recounting of God's faithfulness first gave him and his people courage—even if just enough courage to continue to cry out to Him for help. When I reflect on the evidence of God's history of faithfulness in my own life, it fuels the fire of my prayers.

Andrew: As Trey told me during our night drive, he and Stephanie were pressing in to God hard. Jehoshaphat's examination of God is fair. Trey and Stephanie's questions are fair. God's involvement before, during, and after our hardships is mysterious, and rarely do we get to connect the dots of the spiritual realm. All the more reason to suggest this: if we avoid our doubts, skip the questions, and numb the pain, we stunt surrender and miss discovering more of the Eternal, who exists and responds from an infinite (that is, immeasurably great; unbounded or unlimited) paradigm.

FAST

Andrew: Once Jehoshaphat allows himself to ask the tough questions, his limited understanding is confronted with God's eternal continuum and he asks for help. He also readies Judah and himself for God's response with a fast (v. 3). More than a last-ditch effort to summon help from on high, fasting was Judah's collective sign of surrender. By reserving for prayer the time usually spent eating and drinking, Judah was corporately saying, "You are God. We are not."

My brother and his wife practiced spiritual routines with their young family as a joint abandon to God's agenda. Their toddler girls' selfless prayers to God for "Mommy's" healing was an exercise in *faith* (complete confidence or trust in a person), not feel-good superstition. The girls' conscious trust in a power other than their own was led and echoed by Trey and Stephanie's preceding decision to "press in to God."

"'If we encounter disaster *or disease* . . . You will hear our cries and rescue us.' Now *is the time to ask for your help*" (vv. 9–10). "For we have no power against this great multitude that is coming against us; nor do we know what to do, but our eyes are upon You" (v. 12 NKJV). To learn what the Eternal has up His sleeve, I am convinced that we must confront Him with our doubts and questions, let go of control, and fast for His response. In short, we must surrender— perhaps the most difficult step in discovering what God wants.

Read Psalm 143. David's transparent cry for help from the Eternal still echoes in the chambers of our painful stories today.

WAIT: LISTEN AND POSITION

READ 2 CHRONICLES 20:13–21.

[13]All Judah (*men and* women, children, and infants) were waiting in front of the Eternal's *temple when Jehoshaphat asked this.* [14]There, the Spirit of the Eternal descended on *a Levitical singer,* Jahaziel (son of Zechariah, son of Benaiah, son of Jeiel, son of Mattaniah, a Levite son of Asaph).

Jahaziel: [15]Listen *to me,* all Judah, citizens of Jerusalem, and King Jehoshaphat. The Eternal has responded to your *pleading:* "Do not fear or worry about this army. The battle is not yours to fight; it is the True God's. [16]Tomorrow, they will travel through the ascent of Ziz. Meet them at the end of valley before the wilderness of Jeruel. *There,*

I will be watching. [17]Stand and watch, but do not fight the battle. There, you will watch the Eternal save you, Judah and Jerusalem."

Do not fear or worry. Tomorrow, face the army *and trust that* the Eternal is with you.

[18]Jehoshaphat bowed his head low, and all the assembly fell prostrate before the Eternal and worshiped Him *with reverence. They trusted the Lord completely.* [19]Meanwhile, the Levite families of the Kohathites and Korahites stood up to praise the Eternal One, True God of Israel, with very loud voices.

[20]Early the next morning they went out to the wilderness of Tekoa. There Jehoshaphat's message *to Judah was not about courage in battle.*

Jehoshaphat: Listen to me, Judah and inhabitants of Jerusalem. Trust in the Eternal One, your True God, *not in your own abilities,* and you will be supported. Put your trust in His *words that you heard through the* prophets, and *we will* succeed.

[21]Having addressed his people, Jehoshaphat asked those who sang to the Eternal to lead the army and praise His magnificence and holiness.

Chorus *(singing)*: Give thanks to the Eternal because His loyal love is forever!

LISTEN

Ginny: I met Ronell when she was twenty years old. A Trinidad native, she came to the United States just after her eighteenth birthday, not to conquer the world, but to receive treatment for bone and soft tissue cancer. As time passed, her condition worsened, the cancer was deemed terminal, and Ronell lost a leg and part of a lung. She did not lose her hope, however, or her fervor for life or faith in God.

When I met Ronell, she was in the process of recording an album of her original songs and compiling a book of her own essays and poetry. All her writings were inspired by her life in Trinidad and her battle with cancer. From our first meeting, I was amazed by how much she could get done in a day in spite of being confined to a wheelchair and on ridiculously high doses of medication.

Ronell's dream was to travel the world, share her music and writings, and tell anyone who would listen how she had been healed. Yet she was very aware that her next breath could be her last and that she would find herself in Jesus' arms before any of her earthly dreams had been realized. She would always tell me, "Either way, I win."

And she believed it. During the time I knew Ronell, I watched her suffer, fear, and grow frustrated with the cards she had been dealt. In addition to her big dreams, she wanted the simple things— to be able to run again, to get married and have children, to not be in pain. But her hope was never far away. She poured out her heart to God and to others in her songs and her poetry. Her spirit of surrender was not only encouraging but contagious. I heard countless stories of how Ronell's journey encouraged many to reach out to the God they had turned their backs on or never known.

During our first afternoon together, Ronell and I sat at a piano and in twenty minutes finished writing a song that I had been trying to finish for ten years. The title was "Say Amen." The lyrics were a declaration of surrender to the Lord, no matter the outcome. I'm certain that we were able to finish so quickly because Ronell learned during her battle with cancer what true surrender looked like.

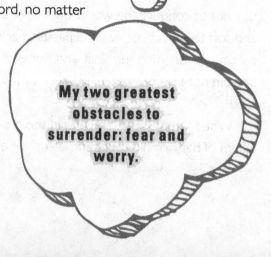

My two greatest obstacles to surrender: fear and worry.

Andrew: I tend to make decisions out of a need to control, fostering an environment of dizzying anxiety. Though I didn't know Ronell, I'm sure her instinct was to try to be healed, to find a solution, to exercise every treatment her body could handle. But through her traumatic journey, she learned to give up control and open her mind to the reality of her situation—perhaps thereby opening her heart to the reality of God.

I have noticed when I decide to stop manipulating things I can't master, when I try to surrender, outside observers with common convictions always show up as an oasis of comfort in my desert of incomprehension. Perhaps similar to how Ginny showed up in Ronell's life. Or maybe even vice versa.

Jehoshaphat, rather than freeze in panic over a predicament he could not control, makes a conscious effort to surrender. And once he surrenders, God speaks through Jahaziel, a Levitical singer (see "Music Matters" sidebar): "Do not fear or worry about this army. The battle is not yours to fight; it is the True God's" (v. 15). Jahaziel's reassuring tune features my two greatest obstacles to surrender: fear and worry.

Jehoshaphat has cause to worry. His kingdom has few if any options to fend off an insurmountable alliance of militants who have marked Judah as the prize. He is in hardcore need of a solution. But Jehoshaphat's prior decision to surrender readies his mind and heart to listen before acting. And Jahaziel's delivery confirms that God has Judah's back, providing the spiritual sustenance Jehoshaphat needs to confidently lead his people into a battle calculated for catastrophic defeat.

"The battle is not yours to fight" (v. 15) resounded through community deeds of encouragement for Ronell and my brother's family—meal deliveries, car rides for my nieces, songwriting sessions for Ronell, and vulnerable private conversations from those who had experienced cancer—tangibly reiterating their daily decision to press in to the Eternal, and their fight against a disease with unpredictable outcomes was reinforced.

POSITION

Andrew: Halfway through his prophetic telegram, Jahaziel further admonishes Judah with concrete instructions. "You will not need to fight in this battle. Position yourselves, stand still and see the salvation of the LORD, who is with you" (v. 17 NKJV). Jehoshaphat heeds Jahaziel's advice and encourages Judah to rely on the infinite nature of the Eternal for success, not his own human capabilities. As a result, Judah's battle cry was a song of thanksgiving rather than murder. And their strategy was faith ("*They trusted the Lord completely*" [v. 18]), not the national military.

From the first signs of ambush, Jehoshaphat has wisely been preparing his mind and heart, as well as the collective mind and heart of his country, for surrender—a disposition contrary to the onset of war. But Judah's spiritual stance is not a symbol of martial weakness, it is an exercise of big picture strength. It is trust in a divine, eternal plan.

You will not need to fight this battle.

As Stephanie strategically positioned her body for healing with tests, surgeries, and chemotherapy treatments, friends' faith-filled support allied with my brother's family in a posture of awestruck surrender to the True God, giving Trey's crew the confidence to "stand still and see the salvation of the LORD, who is with you" (v. 17 NKJV). And they, too, sang songs of thanksgiving as they waited for God to deliver Stephanie from cancer. As Trey told me, they knew that God would heal Stephanie. They just didn't know if He would temporarily heal her body or eternally heal her spirit. These communal acts of faith, much like Judah's corporate fast, gave our extended family the spiritual nutrition to watch and wait with Trey and Stephanie in her very personal fight with cancer.

Waiting is not easy. But once we make the decision to surrender, we listen and position—often with the support of others—in an effort to patiently discover God's character further uncovered through our stories.

BELIEVE: REST AND PONDER

Read 2 Chronicles 20:22–30.

[22]As they sang and praised, the Eternal was ready *to cause great confusion in battle* for the men from Ammon, Moab, and Mount Seir *(in Edom)* who had come to attack Judah. They were utterly defeated, *turning on one another.* [23]The Ammonites and Moabites attacked the men from Mount Seir, destroying them completely. Then, the Ammonites and Moabites turned on each other. [24]When *all was quiet,* Judah looked out of the watchtower in the wilderness and saw a great army of corpses fallen *on the battlefield.* No one had escaped. [25]Then Jehoshaphat and his people took various goods, clothing, and valuables *off the dead bodies and seized the abundant livestock.* There was so much that it took three days to recover it all. [26]On the fourth day, they assembled in the valley of Beracah, where they had blessed the Eternal *and where He had blessed them with a victory,* and named the place, "The Valley of Beracah," as it is still known today.

[27]Every man of Judah and citizen of Jerusalem followed Jehoshaphat back to Jerusalem, joyous because the Eternal defeated their enemies. [28]They paraded into Jerusalem with harps, lyres, and trumpets and up to the Eternal's house.

[29-30]For the rest of his reign, Jehoshaphat's kingdom was peaceful because the Eternal had fought the Southern Kingdom's enemies, making all the surrounding kingdoms fear the True God.

REST

Andrew: Judah trusted the Lord "completely" (v. 18). As is often the case with God and the Old Testament, the spoils go to the underdog who simply believes that God will provide exactly how He says He will. As is displayed throughout Jehoshaphat's story, God is not ignorant of the stress and strain of His people's faithful efforts. "Then the realm of Jehoshaphat was quiet, for his God gave him rest all around" (v. 30 NKJV). God rewarded Judah's belief with peace.

For now, Stephanie is cancer-free. Her hair has grown back. Doctors appointments are less frequent. She can pick up her girls again. In the wake of the stress and strain of cancer, she and her family have been given rest.

Ginny: But peace comes in different forms. Five months after meeting Ronell, I sang our song "Say Amen" at her memorial service. A dark, unfair day had come for those of us who knew and loved her. Different than it was with Trey and Stephanie, our peace came in knowing that she was no longer in pain, that she was united with the One she'd sung her song of surrender to for so long. Her body was not healed. But her spirit was. God honored Ronell by giving her His "rest all around."

PONDER

Andrew: Cancer or no cancer, we are all terminally ill because of sin. Disease, poverty, broken relationships, natural disasters, and a host of other heartaches prove to even the most abstract theological mind that something on this earth has gone awry. Every human experience, no matter how controlled, ends in physical extinction. We all die.

Surrender doesn't explain all the mysteries of God—nor do the stories of Judah and Jehoshaphat or Trey and Stephanie or Ronell. But their trial-tested faiths expose fibers of God's infinite character. And as we discover bits of His character, we grasp better the reality of our wider eternal context. We live our stories not to prove God, but to glorify what it is that He wants. And in that process, we find our identity—and our rest—completely in our Creator.

MUSIC MATTERS

Andrew: One of my greatest insecurities is that my profession doesn't matter, that music is just art designed for whimsical pleasure rather than eternal kingdom impact. Well, the Old Testament proves me wrong.

In 2 Chronicles 20, Jehoshaphat leads his army into battle with musicians singing songs of praise and thanksgiving, a gloriously tangible reminder that Judah's fight is God's fight. Then in verse 22, God uses the musicians to queue His master strategy to deliver Judah from its enemies: "Now when they began to sing and to praise, the Lord set ambushes against the people of Ammon, Moab, and Mount Seir" (NKJV).

Read 2 Samuel 22. David composes a psalm of praise to the Eternal for delivering him from the hands of his enemies.

> We live our stories not to prove God, but to glorify what it is that He wants.

Notice the many characteristics that David uses to describe God in this song.

Read Psalm 32. Even God sings to protect His people.

Q&A:
Thoughtful Prayer

Andrew: How has your prayer life been impacted by reading the Bible?

Ginny: Over the past couple of years, I've been learning the value of surrendering my time to the Lord, a fasting of sorts. For me, this typically means at least an hour of Scripture study and prayer each day. I didn't feel I needed to do this in order to please or appease God. Instead, it was a life change born out of desperation. I desperately needed to know Him more fully. I desperately wanted to learn to pray more thoughtfully and intentionally. Mostly, I desperately needed to gain a deeper sense of the reality that God is God and I am not.

As I've been reading through Scripture, I have been taking time to write a brief summary of what I read as I read it. Again and again, I'm struck by God's faithfulness to His people. I've found this new awareness deeply impacting my prayer life, causing me to conclude that the more I whisper to myself of His goodness and faithfulness, the more I believe He can do beyond what I could ever ask or imagine (Eph. 3:20).

QUESTIONS for Reflection

1. Jehoshaphat saw a huge army coming to attack him, and he was overwhelmed and afraid. When have circumstances in your life made you overwhelmed and afraid? Are you in that situation at present?

2. What does it mean that Jehoshaphat "sought the Eternal" (v. 3)? How does a person seek God, in practical terms? In what areas of your life today do you need to "seek God"?

3. Why is it difficult at times to simply stand still? If you had been in Judah during this time, what would your natural inclination have been? How would you have reacted when God said, "Just stand still and watch"?

4. What battles in your life are too big for you at present? What would it mean, in practical terms, for you to "stand and watch" God fight those battles on your behalf?

MIDNIGHT OF THESE THINGS

(Words and Music: Andrew Greer)

We just found out mama's got the disease
We're still asking why
Just a young family, our little girls
Barely knee high
But in our darker hours
We pray for eyes to see
In the midnight of these things
Praying hard in our hearts
Trying to drown the doubts in our mind
God grant us grace
The harder we search, the less we find
When answers are few and far between
We get down on our knees
In the midnight of these things
O God of mercy, give a little light to see
Grant our hurting hearts just enough faith
To fully believe
The youngest of three
Asks to pray if we'll let her
And with mountains of faith she says
"God, thanks for making mom feel better"
When we're tired or hurting
We hear the angels sing
In the midnight of these things

CHAPTER **2**

SAY AMEN

"When you know you're holding tighter to His hand / That's when you can say amen . . ."

—Ginny Owens and Ronell Ragbir, "Say Amen"

"I believe with all my heart God's Story has a happy ending . . . But not yet, not necessarily yet. It takes faith to hold on to that in the face of the great burden of experience, which seems to prove otherwise."

—Elisabeth Elliot, *Through Gates of Splendor*[1]

Ginny: My dear friend Charlynn and I "met" during our first day in freshman English. The scene is still vivid in my mind. I had arrived early and found a desk in the front row. Charlynn and her BFFs came crashing in just before the professor took attendance. They took seats in the back and whispered and giggled the entire time our professor was lecturing. I distinctly remember thinking, *Who in the world are these obnoxious people?*

I'd soon learn that Char and her crew were the pretty, popular, party girls on campus. I, being the shy wallflower, did not anticipate ever becoming good friends with these girls, but I did soon enough. Charlynn and I especially bonded. We'd do laps around the track for hours, discussing every topic from guys to our future aspirations, to the latest campus gossip, and back to guys again. We had an unusual knack for exploring the very deep and the very

19

shallow in equal measure. And when we'd spent too much time philosophizing, gossiping, and boy-watching, we'd stay up all night studying, and make 4 a.m. snack runs to the Circle K across the street from campus. Not the wisest move for a couple of college girls, but we embraced the risk. It was more dangerous than anything we'd done in our lives up to that point.

There were several reasons Charlynn and I became fast friends. For one, I was not attempting to infiltrate the "In Crowd," so I could be trusted with her secrets and her true self. And though I was milder and quieter than her clan, she accepted me, too, and invited me out of my shell. We were both strong women, used to handling everyone else's problems. For each other, we provided a listening ear and honest feedback, rare finds for that season of life. And last but not least, we both had the same hopes for the future—music careers and families of our own. Charlynn was way ahead on the family idea, with a line of suitors stretching out the door and around the block. I did not have the same fortune. She tried in vain to teach me the secret of making every guy fall in love. I was terrified of the idea of every guy falling in love. And so, she went out on dates, and I went to the piano to brood.

After college, I got a record deal and Charlynn got married. We both had a tough time adjusting to our new lives. In fact, I think it's fair to say that she and I each longed desperately for what the other had. I remember a conversation one day when she was out on the road with me. Her wedding was a few weeks away, and I was lamenting the fact that a relationship didn't seem to be on the horizon for me. She said reproachfully, "Girl, you're the lucky one. Don't you know we'd all put marriage on hold if we could have the career you have?"

Her statement took me by surprise. How could anyone want a career more than marriage? Don't get me wrong; I was certainly independent and headstrong enough to do life alone; I just didn't want to. I'm not sure I ever admitted it aloud, but there was always an expectation somewhere in the back of my mind that I'd find my soul mate during or soon after college. Though I didn't put life on hold, I did live as if settling down was coming soon. Even as I signed my record deal, I was buying dishes and a dining room table that could seat at least eight. When off the road, I loved having friends over for homemade dinners, collecting recipes, baking bread, and nesting as best I could alone.

And lo these many years later, my perspective and circumstances remain largely unchanged. I nest less, and I'm more confident in the knowledge that I don't need another person to complete me, but the desire is still very present.

In the meantime, I've managed to create a history of relationships marked by comedy and tragedy, perfect evenings and awkward moments, and a few instances of thinking I might be headed for "happily ever after." The comedies are, of course, most fun to recount. There was the awkward night when dinner dragged on forever. When my date said, "You'd better clean your plate—I paid for that meal," I finally realized why. How romantic. Needless to say, he did not get a second try.

Then there was the time I refused to go on a blind date when the friend setting it up said, "The great thing is you won't even mind that he's so ugly." Sure I will. I'm that shallow, especially before the first date.

Unfortunately, the tragedies are pretty tragic, especially the ones when I've been responsible for the heartbreak. Confrontation is not my strong suit, so when I'm the only one who knows

Because I've experienced a broken home, I dream of being part of a healthy, whole relationship, and I hope against hope I have the chance.

21

that the right answer is "No," it's almost as agonizing for me as it is the other person.

In addition to making memories, I've also had time to learn a bit about myself. I've discovered that being the child of divorced parents makes for more unusual relationships as an adult. I'm great at being every guy's best friend girl. That's only fun sometimes. I'm slow to trust, but even so, I rarely make wise choices when I finally do. I'm terrified of rejection and very drawn to those who are skilled at it. The need to work through the broken parts of my story has probably slowed down the process of finding a lifelong partner, but it hasn't lessened the longing.

When I think about being married, I don't dream about the wedding, imagine the house with the picket fence, or name the 2.5 kids. (Okay, maybe just a little. Sometimes.) My longing is more of a subtle nudge that shows up during daily activities. I wish that I weren't the only single girl at the dinner table. I wish for a co-conspirator when planning, hosting, and cleaning up after my dinner parties. I long for someone to take care of, to take long autumn walks with, to laugh with, to solve the problems of the world with, and to grow old with. Because I've experienced a broken home, I dream of being part of a healthy, whole relationship, and I hope against hope I have the chance.

Over the course of time, wise friends have gently encouraged that, "It only takes one. And God's timing will be perfect in bringing that one along." Great. I hear all that, and I have plenty to do in the meantime: my life is full with work and community. My closest friends are a collage of married couples, single girls like me, and great guys who seem to be settled in their bachelorhood. And though I love my life and adore my friends, I must confess that my circumstances feel a bit settled, fixed, and—dare I say—hopeless. I try not to think too much about it, but in the still moments, I can't help but wistfully wonder if a change will ever come.

UNFULFILLED LONGING: THE CONDITION AND THE QUESTION

READ 1 SAMUEL 1:1-8.

When the judges ruled over Israel, there was a man from Ramathaim-zophim, from the hill country of Ephraim. He was Elkanah, who descended from Jeroham, Elihu, Tohu, and Zuph, an Ephraimite. [2]He had two wives: Peninnah, who bore him sons and daughters, and Hannah, who remained childless.

[3]Elkanah used to go up every year from his city to worship and offer sacrifices at the altar of the Eternal One, Commander of *heavenly* armies, at Shiloh, where the priests of the Eternal were Eli's two sons, Hophni and Phinehas. [4]On the days he made a sacrifice, Elkanah would share a portion *of his offering* with his wife Peninnah and all her children, [5]but he offered a double portion *of sacrificial meat* for Hannah because he loved her even though the Eternal One had not given her children. [6]Peninnah used to infuriate Hannah until Hannah trembled with irritation because the Eternal had not given Hannah children. [7]This went on year after year; and every time Hannah went up to the house of the Eternal, Peninnah would infuriate her. So, *as she often did,* Hannah wept and refused to eat.

Elkanah *(seeing Hannah's despair)*: [8]Why are you crying and not eating? Why are you so sad, *Hannah?* Don't I love you more than any 10 sons could?

THE CONDITION

Ginny: The book of 1 Samuel opens with an Israelite people who have been violent, reckless, and immoral for several hundred years. Judges have governed the people, but even they have been corrupt. As a result, everyone does what seems right to them (Judg. 21:25).

Though this phase of Israel's history will draw to a close, there is still at least a half-century of corruption and confusion in the land. Interestingly enough, the backdrop for the picture of dysfunction is the tabernacle in Shiloh, a place where people are supposed to come to worship the Eternal.

We are introduced to Elkanah, a devout man from Ephraim who is likely in the minority of Israelites making the yearly trek to Shiloh to offer sacrifices. In spite of his devotion to God, he has adopted a practice that was immoral (though not uncommon) even in his day: polygamy. As Adam Clarke's Bible Commentary states, "wherever there was more than one wife, we find the peace of the family greatly disturbed."[2]

Some scholars believe that Hannah was Elkanah's first wife, and though he loved her immensely, he married Peninnah when they discovered that Hannah could not have children. Peninnah gives birth to many sons and daughters, but Elkanah still loves Hannah more. Talk about a story fraught with unfulfilled longing. One man, two wives. Peninnah, whose name means "jewel" or "pearl," has what every Hebrew woman longs for: children. Hannah, whose name means "settled" or "fixed," has what Peninnah wants: the favor of her husband—but she is infertile.

For a Hebrew woman, being able to have children held a different weight of importance than it does for women in today's Western culture. In Hebrew society, having children, particularly sons, was a wife's defining work. The more men in a family, the more workers for the family. The more sons birthed, the more

> For a Hebrew woman, being able to have children held a different weight of importance than it does for women in today's Western culture.

honorable a woman became in the eyes of her husband and society at large. And in a spiritual context, a barren Hebrew woman was often viewed as cursed by God.

When Elkanah and his family make their annual pilgrimage to Shiloh, the presiding priests are Eli and his two notoriously evil sons, Hophni and Phinehas. Eli has, in his old age, turned a blind eye to all the corruption that his boys indulge in. Later, these two will cause the death of their dad and will lead Israel into a losing battle. But for now, they're busy wreaking havoc on the tabernacle. Adding to the unsettling atmosphere of a house designed for worship over-seen by immoral priests, Elkanah's polygamy makes every worship experience a family disaster. Hannah must spend the journey to and from Shiloh, as well as her time there, surrounded by many chil-dren—none of whom are hers. And Peninnah must simply stand by as her husband falls more and more in love with Hannah. These two miserable women are each other's only peer companionship, and they can't even stand each other (v. 6).

Peninnah was favored by society. Hannah was favored by her husband. And drama ensues.

The Voice translation says that Peninnah would infuriate Han-nah until she "trembled with irritation" (v. 6). The New King James Version says that Peninnah "provoked Hannah severely, to make her miserable." The Hebrew word *ra'am* is used for Peninnah's actions towards Hannah and in every other instance throughout Scripture describes the roar of God's voice or the roar of the seas. And the Hebrew word used for Hannah's weeping is *bakah*, which means to wail in grief, as if for the dead.[3]

It sounds as if Peninnah's taunts are not subtle. She is cruel and ferocious. And Hannah is not whimpering out of frustration but yowling in agony and utter despair. Her unfulfilled longing has almost destroyed her, and her rival's taunts only slice the cut deeper. Year after year, "settled" Hannah feels her curse through Peninnah's pointed jabs. She can't take it anymore. She is losing hope.

While visiting New York City recently, I found myself in a conversation about singleness with Carolyn, a wonderful woman in her late fifties who had just married for the first time. She shared with me several humorous and tragic stories that lined her single path, and then concluded by saying, "I didn't give up completely on the idea of marriage. I just decided it hurt too much to hope."

Boy, did that resonate with me. I don't remember a specific day when I decided that it hurt too much to hope; instead, it was a subtle move. As it became clearer that a lifelong relationship might be far off in the distance, I let my music career consume nearly all my time and slowly began to engage less with my community. Worse still, I gave up praying for a husband because it seemed that God wasn't interested in fulfilling that longing, or perhaps it just wasn't time. In any case, I figured He'd send the right guy along when and if He wanted. Focusing more on work and less on prayer and friends didn't feel like a major decision at first, but over time it spiraled into decisions that had tremendous negative impact on my life. I'd come home from the road and grab a quick dinner out with friends instead of connecting in more meaningful ways. I spent more and more of my time with music industry associates who were most interested in being seen. I was engaging in shallow relationships and abandoning accountability.

As I stopped talking to God about the thing I desired most, I slowly began to talk to Him less about everything else. The

When I consider the thing I think I want most in life, I am much less desperate for it when I realize that my heart will never be completely satisfied by it.

season grew darker. I ended up in a relationship that would eventually bring me lots of heartache and regret. The effects would take years to work through. I understand now that my downward spiral began when I decided that it hurt too much to hope.

Hannah is headed down the path of hopelessness. Her desire for a thing she cannot have has all but consumed her. She is enslaved by it, overwhelmed by it.

As I reflect on Hannah's plight, I consider how unfulfilled longing is a condition we are all burdened by. Because we are separated from God, we desire things that He in His infinite wisdom is not willing to prescribe. And because we want things we can't have, we live with a pervasive restlessness in our souls, and our longings are magnified by the chaos around us.

For Hannah, polygamy and societal expectations cause her agony to increase. For me, growing up without the day-to-day presence of my dad and the expectations of southern culture added to the weight of my longing. Since I can't get past what I want, and I can't physically touch the Eternal or audibly hear His voice, I tend to get caught up in pursuing my lesser longings.

As I consider Hannah's story and my experience this far, I'm left contemplating this broken state and disconnection with God that will be part of our existence until we finally come face to face with Him. And perhaps the way we face this brokenness, these wounds, is to acknowledge it and fight to keep it from possessing our lives. In other words, when I consider the thing I think I want most in life, I am much less desperate for it when I realize that my heart will never be completely satisfied by it. As C. S. Lewis said, "If I find in myself a desire which no experience in this world can satisfy, the most probable explanation is that I was made for another world."[4]

THE QUESTION

Ginny: As I study Hannah's circumstances, I feel that her longing goes so far beyond just desiring a son. Doesn't she also want to belong and to do her part as a wife? Doesn't she want to be defined by something other than childlessness, her rival's taunts, or her husband's affections? How does she find satisfaction and peace in a world that is broken? I know my unfulfilled longing encompasses more than just desiring a husband. I want to love completely and be loved completely. But is that possible in this life?

Hannah is on her way to discovering what she truly longs for, but in her broken state she is unable to notice any of the good things in her life. She can't receive or reciprocate her husband's love. She can't enjoy the feast he has laid before her. And she can't worship.

Elkanah poses a question to Hannah—a question that inspires her to action: "Why are you crying and not eating? Why are you so sad, *Hannah?* Don't I love you more than any 10 sons could?" (v. 8).

Sometimes a simple question is all it takes to motivate a change in direction. I was more than six months into a relationship I should never have been in, and Charlynn simply posed the challenge: "What in the world are you doing, Ginny?" She proceeded to share with me the frog-in-water analogy, which I'd never heard. "If you put a frog in hot water, it will immediately jump out," she retold the classic anecdote. "But if you put a frog in cool water and heat it up slowly, it will stay in and die."

I understood. I was boiling in a bad relationship and dying because I was enslaved to my longing. During the conversation, Charlynn's last question went something like this: "Don't you know if you keep going in this direction, you will lose in the end?"

Hannah is also on the brink of dying in her hopelessness. She must decide what to do with her unfulfilled longing. Will she let her relationship with her husband be enough? Will she remain wretched? If not, where will she find hope? Instead of responding to Elkanah's question, Hannah makes a different choice.

SURRENDER: THE POURING OUT AND THE RESTORATION

READ 1 SAMUEL 1:9–18.

9–10One day after they ate and drank at Shiloh, Hannah got up *and presented herself before the Lord.* It so happened that the priest Eli was sitting *in a place of honor* beside the doorpost of the Eternal's congregation tent *as Hannah entered.* She was heartbroken, and she began to pray to the Eternal One, weeping uncontrollably as she did.

Hannah: 11Eternal One, Commander of *heavenly* armies, if only You will look down at the misery of Your servant and remember me—oh, don't forget me!—and give Your servant a son, then I promise I will devote the boy to Your service *as a Nazirite* all the days of his life. [He will never touch wine or other strong drink,] and no razor will ever cut his hair.

12As she prayed *silently* before the Eternal One, *the priest* Eli watched her mouth: 13Hannah's lips were moving, but since she was praying silently, he could not hear her words. So Eli thought she was drunk.

Eli: 14How long are you going to continue drinking, *making a spectacle of yourself?* Stop drinking wine, *and sober up!*

Hannah: 15My lord, I am not drunk on wine or any strong drink; I am just a woman with a wounded spirit. I have been pouring out *the pain in* my soul before the Eternal One. 16Please don't consider your servant some worthless woman just because I have been speaking for so long out of worry and exasperation.

Eli: [17]Go, don't worry about this anymore, and may the True God of Israel fulfill the petition you have made to Him.

Hannah: [18]May your servant be favored in your sight.

Then Hannah rose and went back to where she was staying. The sadness lifted from her, so she was able to eat.

THE POURING OUT

Ginny: I do not understand how prayer works. But the longer I live, the more childlike my view of prayer becomes. I pray to get through each day, and I cope with circumstances by praying through them—because I must. Hannah seems to be at that point as well. Though she is considered a woman of great faith, it seems that at this point in her journey, at wit's end, she is simply a broken woman pouring out her heart to the Eternal God whom she and her family serve. In desperation, with tears and whispers, Hannah moves towards the Eternal. Prayer is not passive. Prayer requires action on our part: engagement, reflection, surrender.

I remember when desperation finally gave way to surrender in my journey. After nearly a year of being in a relationship laced with compromise, God delivered me. The thing I feared finally came to pass—total and complete rejection. I had been abandoned for someone else, and the message had been delivered in the most cold, unemotional manner. The doors of possibility for our future had been slammed shut and locked. I knew it was a blessing because I may never have found the strength to leave otherwise. But it felt like a nightmare. My heart was in such disarray that I couldn't imagine how to begin putting the pieces back together. In that season, I learned to pray desperate prayers, and I learned to be transparent with others. I had no choice. I couldn't manage alone.

Hannah can't manage alone anymore, either. She wastes no time in getting to the point of her prayer. That's how it is when we're desperate, isn't it? She begins by acknowledging to God and to herself His ability to change her circumstances and confesses her heart's desire: "Eternal One, Commander of *heavenly* armies, if only You will look down at the misery of Your servant and remember me . . . and give Your servant a son" (v. 11).

Hannah's prayer is simple, forthright, and honest, prompting me to consider that prayer isn't a place to be polite but a space for communion with God, where I can lay everything before Him in expectation that He will do "immeasurably more than all we ask or imagine" (Eph. 3:20 NIV). If I could own and name in prayer the desires of my heart, I wonder how life would change.

After asking the Eternal for a son, Hannah makes an unthinkable promise to the Lord: "I promise I will devote the boy to Your service *as a Nazirite* all the days of his life" (v. 11).

Usually, when I ask the Lord for something, I don't consider giving it back to Him. But not Hannah. If she is attempting to negotiate with God, the deal she's asking for doesn't work in her favor. If her son is to be a Nazirite surrendered to God's service, he won't be hers for long. He won't be around for her to show off. He won't add to the workforce or the wealth of the family. Hannah is doing much more than asking God for a son; she is com-mitting herself to the tremendous sacrifice of giving back the gift she is praying so desperately for. She is surrendering to Him the thing she wants most.

What has happened during this short prayer? I can't help but think that as Hannah has poured

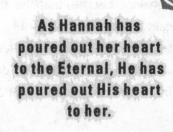

As Hannah has poured out her heart to the Eternal, He has poured out His heart to her.

out her heart to the Eternal, He has poured out His heart to her. Is it possible that God also has unfulfilled longing? A longing to commune with His people? Is that desire somehow reflected in Hannah's desperation?

Scripture records that He closed her womb (v. 5 NKJV). Did He close her womb so that they would have this moment of communion? So that she would pour out her heart and catch a glimpse of His? As she discovered who the Eternal is, was she compelled to surrender to Him the thing that she longed most for, engaging herself in a much greater story that satisfied much greater longings than her current request?

In the twenty-second lesson of the classic book on prayer, *With Christ in the School of Prayer,* author Andrew Murray writes, "Prayer is not monologue, but dialogue; God's voice in response to mine is its most essential part."[5] I can't know for sure what happened during Hannah's prayer. But I find enough evidence in my own life of the power of prayer to change heart direction to think that somehow Hannah's life and heart were also transformed. Perhaps the act of surrendering our deepest longings to God is enough to bring about change. But I think God is more present in our prayers than this.

THE RESTORATION

Ginny: Several sources note that Hannah is the first person mentioned in the Bible who has offered a private prayer in public. Eli, never having seen such behavior, assumes that she is drunk and calls her out on it (v. 13–14). He is used to corrupt behavior in the temple and imagines that Hannah is no different. But in her "poured out" state, she

God continually shows me that those closest to me are tangible representations of His speaking in my life.

is uninhibited, devoid of pride, and without hesitation or frustration tells her story to Eli. "I am just a woman with a wounded spirit. I have been pouring out *the pain in* my soul before the Eternal One" (v. 15). There is something restorative about confession for both the confessor and the listener.

After my breakup, I found peace when I poured out my heart in prayer and confessed to those I trusted. Surrendering my brokenness and acknowledging my mistakes were humbling but hopeful, reminding me of my inability to conquer life on my own. That dark season gave me a deeper understanding of my need to be vulnerable with others. Prayer is priority. But God continually shows me that those closest to me are tangible representations of His speaking in my life.

As the listener, I often find the confessions of others humbling, challenging me to evaluate my level of honesty. The humility that Hannah displays as she shares her heart moves Eli. He, too, lives in the midst of a tragedy. He is nearly blind to such faithfulness because it's been absent for so long, perhaps even in his own life. So upon hearing Hannah's heart, Eli pronounces a blessing over her: "May the True God of Israel fulfill the petition you have made to Him" (v. 17).

Now, after baring her soul to the Eternal and Eli, Hannah's despair lifts and she is finally able to eat and worship with her family (v. 18–19). The Eternal has responded to Hannah's prayer by replacing her misery with peace. Hannah's surrender has led to freedom. Eli's blessing has left her encouraged.

Andrew: As I listen to the confessional conversations inside Ginny's story and her discovery of the spiritual healthiness and importance of connecting with others through our doubts and pains, I instantly relate. The notion that we are designed to be in communion with each other has been reiterated over and over in my life experiences.

As the exchange between Eli and Hannah illustrates, everyone is welcome at the table of God—Eli the spiritual leader, Hannah the wailing wonderer. As we seek to connect with each other—multicultural, multiethnic, multidenominational, and yes, multireligious—we play an impactful part in praying and playing out Jesus' New Testament prayer, "on earth as it is in heaven" (Matt. 6:10 NIV). Our semantics may be all screwy, our backgrounds diluted and dysfunctional, and our pride swollen with fear and hurt, but at the table of God, everyone is welcome. Everybody.

Sure we have conversations. We engage in discourse and disagreement. We flat out don't understand each other and get frustrated and annoyed. But as we sup at the same spread, God speaks. And I am convinced that He uses our willingness and our wants to relate with each other to engage in His conversations with each of us individually.

Many of my friends who are Christ-followers express their confusion concerning, and fear of, how to interact with our neighbors of different religious persuasions. My responsive question is always, "Aren't we all human inside the heart?" We all have this human condition. We are all housed in this painfully temporal structure, pining steadfastly and sometimes recklessly for an eternal home with our mysterious yet drawing Creator.

Perhaps if we were more open to be involved in each other's lives despite our discomfort with our different traditions and practices, God could use our various stories to hone us in together on the one true God to experience confession and communion together—the kingdom of God—forever.

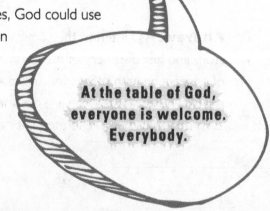

At the table of God, everyone is welcome. Everybody.

RESPONSE TO BLESSING: SACRIFICE AND SONG

READ 1 SAMUEL 1:19—2:2.

¹⁹The next morning, they rose early to worship the Eternal One. Then they went back to their home at Ramah, and Elkanah slept with Hannah his wife. The Eternal remembered her *petition;* ²⁰and in the new year, Hannah became pregnant. When her son was born, she named him Samuel, *which means "His name is El (God),"* because she said,

Hannah: I asked the Eternal One for him.

²¹*The next year,* Elkanah and all his family went up *to Shiloh* to make their sacrifices to the Eternal and to fulfill his vow. ²²But Hannah remained behind.

Hannah *(to Elkanah)***:** When the child can eat solid food, I will bring him so that he can appear in the presence of the Eternal One and remain there continually.

Elkanah *(to Hannah)***:** ²³Do whatever you think best. If you want to wait until Samuel is weaned, do that. Since the Eternal is faithful, surely He will keep His word.

So Hannah stayed at home and nursed her son until he was weaned. ²⁴When that day came, she gathered a three-year-old bull, over half a bushel of flour, and a skin of wine; and she took him to the house of the Eternal One at Shiloh. Samuel was just a lad. ²⁵They slaughtered the bull, and they brought the child to *the priest* Eli.

Hannah *(to Eli)***:** ²⁶My lord, I swear I am the woman who was praying to the Eternal One in front of you. ²⁷It was this child I prayed for, and the Eternal has indeed granted me the petition I made. ²⁸So, *as I vowed,* I will lend him back to the Eternal. For as long as he lives, let him serve our Eternal One.

And she left Samuel there *with Eli* to serve the Eternal One.

CHAPTER 2

Then Hannah prayed *out of her deepest feelings.*

Hannah: My heart rejoices in the Eternal One;
      my strength grows strong in the Eternal.
My mouth can mock my enemies
      because I celebrate how You have saved me!

  ²No one is holy like the Eternal One—
      no, no one but You;
      and there is no rock *as solid* as our True God.

SACRIFICE

Ginny: Hannah's prayer is answered when the Eternal blesses her with a son. She names him Samuel, which means "Asked of God" or "Lent by God." She has not forgotten who gave her Samuel or the promise she made to Him.

During the annual journey to Shiloh, Hannah could have taken Samuel to worship with her family. If I were in her place, I would have been tempted to carry him up to the temple to display him for Peninnah and everyone else to see. She is now a mother, after all. But she stays behind. And I'm sure that as a mother she wants to bond with her son before surrendering him indefinitely. But I also suspect that she has nothing to prove and no longer needs to be defined by having a child. The object of her longing has changed.

Over time, the object of my longing has changed as well. God has opened my eyes to the reality that true peace can only be found in pursuing Him. In theory, I've always known this. But now I'm beginning to experience it firsthand. As much as I long for a husband, I have accepted with hope that today is not that day. And if the day comes, said husband will not be able to satisfy the deepest longing in my soul. It would be devastating for both of us if he were forced to try. That is a space that only the Eternal is capable of filling. So I spend my time and energy on the things He places in my path: enjoying my colorful group of friends, embracing my freedom, and taking advantage of the hours I have alone. I don't ignore my longing anymore. I give it to the Eternal daily, fully aware that if my circumstances change, the need to constantly surrender them will not.

When Samuel is just a young boy, Hannah and Elkanah gather their offerings and their young son and go up to Shiloh. After offering their sacrifices to the Eternal, they bring their precious child to Eli. As Hannah places her son in Eli's care, she shares with him the testimony that the Eternal has changed her heart and life and has given her Samuel (v. 27–28).

What if Hannah's story had been typical and she had borne children like Peninnah? Perhaps she would have worshiped the Eternal, but the desperate need to cry out to Him would have been missing. In that case, her barrenness wouldn't have produced a fertile meeting place for God. She wouldn't have surrendered this promise to Him. And she certainly wouldn't be offering this joyful sacrifice now.

Commentary from The Voice Bible says, "Hannah's prayers for a child, her absolute faith in God's plan, and her willingness to be a part of it however she can, resonate as the kings and warriors begin to enter the stage."

Hannah has given Samuel to God, and God will raise him up as a faithful priest who will follow His ways and crown the first two kings of Israel. This is probably far more than Hannah could ever fathom. And rarely will we witness how our sacrifices play a part in the Eternal's bigger story.

In the story of Hannah, a longing surrendered becomes a blessing, and a blessing surrendered becomes a song.

THE SONG

Ginny: If my journey had been different, my songs would have been different as well. If I had gotten married right after college, perhaps there would have been no time or space for songs at all. I am certain that much of my songwriting has been born out of the broken places, the prayers, and the quiet where God has met me.

In the story of Hannah, a longing surrendered becomes a blessing, and a blessing surrendered becomes a song. As Hannah gives her only child to God, she celebrates. No sadness is recorded, only praise and prophetic words. It seems that just as God responded to Hannah's sorrowful prayer, He sings in her exuberant song. Hannah celebrates how He has saved her (2:1). She testifies to His greatness (v. 2). And she marvels at the mysteries of His power to change all circumstances: breaking the strong and strengthening the feeble (v. 4), giving food to the hungry, and giving children to the barren woman (v. 5). Her encounter with the Eternal has changed her heart forever. And His miracle gift to her gives Hannah firsthand knowledge of His power.

My story does not read like Hannah's, but her song inspires a question in me: *What is the song my heart sings?* Have I invited the Eternal so deep into my desperation that my song sings of His hope? Have I reveled in His goodness enough that my song sings of His glory? From the broken parts of our stories, the best songs emerge. Even when God does not give us the things we desire the most, if He has met us, then He has moved in us and given us Himself. And for the gift of Him we have reason to sing with Hannah: "My heart rejoices in the Eternal One; my strength grows strong in the Eternal. . . . No one is holy like the Eternal One—no, no one but You" (vv. 1–2).

Q&A:
Why Music?

Ginny: Personally speaking, how did songwriting become a part of your life?

Andrew: Music has always been the medium I am most comfortable using to communicate my story. Whether a story about an outcome of a relationship or my doubts about God, songs have given me an outlet to express my most introverted thoughts. I suspect this is true for most songwriters and performers.

I didn't begin to craft songs until life really began to happen, a year or so after college. When the stuff hit the fan. You know—you have lived through those messy seasons. When my feelings were so exposed and unexplainable, I took to songwriting. So I guess it is no surprise that music has such a definitive place in the stories of the lives affected by God in the Old Testament. If I had been Hannah, I would have begun crafting hits the moment I exited the temple in emotional upheaval.

Whether celebration or lament, praise is the voice of longing— longings both fulfilled and unfulfilled. Worship is motivated by our thankful hearts, and music helps compose the praise that worship births. For the rest of my life, whenever I am living in benchmarks of my spiritual journey, I will always take to the ivories with my pen and paper in tow.

> **Whether celebration or lament, praise is the voice of longing.**

CHARACTER SONGS

Ginny: God's ways are higher than ours, which gives our circumstances conclusions that are the opposite of what we expect. He gives Hannah, a barren woman, a child who will serve His people. And in the New Testament, He gives Mary, a virgin, a child who will change the world. Because of these miraculous conceptions, Hannah and Mary both sing songs of praise, thankfulness, and prophecy. Explore Hannah's prayer in 1 Samuel 2:1–10 and Mary's prayer in Luke 1:46–55. Note the striking similarities between the two prayer songs. Both speak of the mysterious aspects of God's character and His way of doing things that seems upside-down to our human perspective—humbling the proud, lifting up the humble, feeding the hungry, and remembering His people.

QUESTIONS for Reflection

1. What factors contribute to Hannah's deep grief and sorrow? When have you experienced sorrow at things that were beyond your control? How did the words or actions of others contribute to your sorrow?

2. How did Hannah's anguish affect others around her? If you were in her position, how would you have responded to Elkanah's attempts at consolation (v. 8)? At his extravagant demonstrations of love (v. 5)?

3. Put yourself in Peninnah's place: why do you think she tormented Hannah (v. 6)? If you were Hannah, how would you have responded?

4. If you were Hannah, how would you have responded to God for your barrenness? What situations in your own life experiences have made you wonder if God was paying attention?

5. When have you rejoiced in faith that God was going to answer your prayer—even before the answer came?

SAY AMEN

(Words and Music: Ginny Owens and Ronell Ragbir)

When the burdens of your life feel so heavy
And the shadows of your past won't let go
When the world around you seems to be so lonely
And you feel that there's no hope
Say amen
When you cannot bear your cross alone
When you realize you're not on your own
And when all your pride is finally gone
Say Amen
When the only thing you have is faith
You know that every step you take
Is leading you to His embrace
When you know you're holding tighter to His hand
That's when you can say amen
I've known many troubles in my lifetime
And I have heard death knocking at my door
But in my darkest hour of desperation
I call out to the One who calms the storm
When your heart cries out for love
When your soul is torn and bruised
Just surrender to the One
Who was broken for you

CHAPTER 3

RESCUE ME

"Please don't be afraid to show your glorious face / And hold our hands in the dark / We're hoping that your nearness / Might be enough forgiveness for all our many wrongs . . ."

—Andrew Greer, "Rescue Me"

"I used to think God wouldn't talk to me when I was confused, but now I think he was just listening."

—Bob Goff, *Love Does*[1]

"The essence of Christianity . . . is the message of the eternally other, the one who is far above the world, yet who from the depth of the divine being has mercy on the person who gives glory to him alone."

—Dietrich Bonhoeffer, "Jesus Christ and the Essence of Christianity"[2]

Andrew: I wish I possessed more courage, that I was strong enough to allow what I believe with my mind to sink into my heart and change the ways I live. As an adult, I have seen firsthand the beautiful and grotesque play out in the lives of my circumference of community. I have been honored to walk alongside and intimately witness the experiences of others in their darkest hours. And through witnessing these midnight experiences, I have become acutely aware of how deeply God loves and is one hundred percent for people— for my friends, for my family, yes, even for my foes.

Yet I still wonder if God loves *me*. This belief that God has created everyone but me worthy of His attention is a prickly thorn in my flesh called pride. I don't generally consider myself a person who is ostracized by pride—though that statement alone may be rather prideful. My mind's rationale, built on observing the lives of those around me, says, *Of course God loves you! He befriended you in Jesus,* but my heart still fears that He can accept everyone's struggle but my own.

Since I was a preteen, I have spent my years as a love addict, a codependent, a compulsive. The upside to being so compulsive? I'm super-focused and productive on positive things: my career and helping others. I am constantly seeking ways to make the former (my career) a generator for the latter (helping others). Not a terrible expenditure of my time, right? But the downside to compulsive behaviors is that I'm super-focused and productive on *negative* things too: unhealthy habits and relationships and low self-esteem—the latter (low self-esteem) viciously generating the former (unhealthy habits and relationships).

Before my inner Eeyore gets all the glory, it must be said that I live a good life. My relationships are profoundly gracious. My family can name every skeleton in my closet, and yet they prepare a plate for me at the table as if my ugly messes are part of what makes my placemat beautiful. My parents have always communicated that in the fellowship of our family, I belong; and not because they have the capacity to love me perfectly, but because God only can love each of us, all of us, perfectly.

Slowly what I believe in my mind trickles down into my heart.

I have a community of faith that keeps me accountable. Some of these folks are confidants in the details of

> **This belief that God has created everyone but me worthy of His attention is a prickly thorn in my flesh called pride.**

my struggles and keep me in check with the utmost intent and grace, reminding me day in and day out that God thinks I am okay, flaws and all. Some of these friends express my value simply by showing their love for me whenever we meet, offering divine levity at just the right moment of spiritual heaviness, often completely unbeknownst to them.

Gradually, what I have learned to be true about God for others is true for me.

I have a job I love. When I am creating, recording, performing, or collaborating in music, it is easy to trust that God thinks of me positively. The creativity He imbues in my innermost being discloses that He cares and participates actively in the details of my life.

Thank God for music. Eventually, the strains of His love sound less like a controlled performance and more like a spontaneous composition.

Ten years ago, I received a Bachelor of Music (BM) from Belmont University in Nashville, Tennessee. I can't remember my exact GPA, but by the single strand of yellow cords adorning my graduation gown, I assume that my academic experience was a mild success—or the university office wanted to squeeze a few dimes out of me for decoration before finally graduating.

Post-graduation, I began working for a record label. Two years later, due to the financial woes of the music industry, I was laid off. I had a hankering for building my own music career, so the job loss was a gift in disguise, but a point of transition nonetheless.

A few months earlier I had entered the world of private counseling, group therapy, and twelve-step meetings after a series of circumstances left me scared of my addiction, wondering if it would eventually leave me spiritually, emotionally, and physically dead. Finally confronting my demons head-on dug up some hope in my heart. But the truths exposed in my counseling sessions of what I believed about God and myself—and how those skewed beliefs manifested in unhealthy behaviors—were sobering, and the effort was necessary to change my perspective and build a library of necessary resources for help.

Stacked on top of these life changes were a few unpleasant relationship experiences, including the loss of a lifelong friend. Though I was experiencing the benefits of fresh therapy, spiritually I felt like my back was up against the wall. Too much too fast. My emotions couldn't keep up and I needed a break.

Nature has always facilitated a vital environment for me to hash it out with God. A hike is a sanctuary where God's presence is no longer a cliché but reality. Outside of city life, my heart feels open and my mind feels clear enough to process, think, and pray. At this point, my heart felt tight and my head dizzyingly full, so I packed up my X-Terra and headed west to spend several months working, playing, and praying in Wyoming.

GOD IS LOVE: MERCY AND I LOVE YOU, NOT IN SPITE OF

READ ISAIAH 54:1–8.

> **Eternal One:** Sing, childless woman, you who have never
> given birth.
> Raise a joyful shout, you who have never gone through labor.
> You, whose husband is dead, will bring forth much more than the
> fertile one who has a husband.
> ²Enlarge your house. You are going to need a bigger place;
> don't underestimate the amount of room that you'll need.
> So build, build, build.
> ³You will increase in every direction *to fill the world.*
> Your offspring will take over the nations;
> Your people will revitalize long-abandoned towns.
>
> ⁴Don't be afraid, for there is no one to shame you.

Don't fear humiliation, for there is no one to disgrace you.
The shame of your younger years and the sorrow of your widow-
      hood are over.
    You'll forget those days *as if they never happened.*
5Because the One who made you will be your husband;
    the One called Commander of *heavenly* armies
Will set you right again, the Holy One of Israel.
    It's not for nothing that He is called "God of all the earth."

6For the Eternal has called you *to come back home,*
    like a young wife, once deserted and deeply injured.
Now God is pulling you close again. *Like a spouse forgives,*
    He will take you back *and be reconciled.*
The Eternal, your Redeemer, says this:

Eternal One: 7*Yes, I was angry* for a moment, and I rejected you,
    but My love endures, and I want you back.
8For that moment, when I was so mad,
    I made it impossible for you to see Me, to find Me,
But with great tenderness, I will take you back in love.

MERCY

Andrew: The Israelites know the wilderness well. They habitually seek out the desert. Consciously or subconsciously—or through a toxic mixture of both—their intentions are diverted from Yahweh, the one who has been, is, and will always be with them, to temporary fixtures: idols, demigods, cultural trends, passive pleasures. "God's people" have a corporate addiction to heeding unhealthy advice and acting out accordingly. Fickle devotion rather than concerted discipleship has marked their history with low lows. I can relate.

My own intentions are easily deflected by the luster of immediate gratification. My addictions toy with my mind and influence my heart to believe that temporary solutions are permanent fixes. From the most benign relationship to the most malignant habit, I am an Israelite. I worship idols because I forget that God loves me. Yet God says, "Mercy."

In Isaiah 54, the Eternal One does not bring down the hammer of consequential judgment. In our sprint for what feels good for the moment, He enters the marathon of redemption. In this prophetic refrain, God saves Isaiah time and speaks directly to the Israelites— to the fruitless womb (v. 1), to me. Throughout my reading of the Old and New Testaments, and in my experience with life, God delivers pardons personally. He doles out mercy with individual kindness. He bestows grace upon grace upon grace, not just for everybody, but for each and every *one*.

Some translators have subtitled Isaiah 54 as "The Future Glory of Zion" (NIV). This title makes sense to me because in these lines God is revealing the core of His character: love through mercy. He borrows our self-constructed dead-end blueprints, refashions them into a holistic master plan, and gives them back for nothing in return. Nothing.

I trekked out to Wyoming with one prayer on my lips: "God, show up or don't. I just have to know." I wasn't angry with God. I couldn't resent or be frustrated by a deity I was not even certain existed. And because I did not project all of my personal issues on Him (a learned skill from an upbringing that taught me to take responsibility for how I behaved and to respond to my circumstances rather than blame God or others), I remained open to the possibility that I might indeed discover Him whispering among the forests of Wyoming and the wildernesses of my heart.

> God, the Redeemer, sent His silky mare back to the barn so He could get down in the mud with you and me.

The scene sounds romantic—but ask anyone I have dated: I'm not much of a romantic. God, the Warrior, splendid on a white horse, never enticed me to seek out or invest in a relationship with Him. The pageantry of gallantry is not real life. Yes, I believe He is supreme and the elements of the universe are on His calling card. But in my experience, more than anything, I believe He cares for people just like you and just like me. In Isaiah 54, God is getting in the middle of the Israelites' mess and countering their flaws with His character of merciful love. God, the Redeemer, sent His silky mare back to the barn so He could get down in the mud with you and me.

Because I think and hope and trust that God knows exactly who He is and is not insecure about Himself, He can quietly, graciously, and lovingly interact with us as the meek "Man of Sorrows" (Isa. 53:3 NKJV). In the middle of our depression, He can come down low to be "grief's patient friend." In the midst of my mayhem, He loves me right where I am.

Never has a more beautiful picture been painted of God, the Liberator, in modern times than in C. S. Lewis's savior-protagonist Aslan in *The Lion, the Witch, and the Wardrobe*. A lion, majestic and fierce, Aslan exhibits his strength in gracious restraint. Mr. Beaver, one of the book's characters, says of Aslan's just love, "Wrong will be right, when Aslan comes in sight. At the sound of his roar, sorrows will be no more. When he bares his teeth, winter meets its death. And when he shakes his mane, we shall have spring again."[3]

Ginny: While Andrew ventured into the woods to find God, I moved to the city. Nearly a year after enduring a difficult breakup (see "Say Amen" chapter) and a month after Ronell lost her fight with cancer, I moved to New York City and enrolled in fiction writing courses at Columbia University. Having fulfilled an eight-year contract with my record label, and having spent those years working nonstop, I was burned out and in need of the anonymity that a smaller town like Nashville just can't provide. Even more desperately, I wanted to hear from God. Though I was searching for what my next steps would be personally, I wanted to spend time getting to know who God is. The noise of my circumstances had drowned out His voice in my life, and like Andrew, my plea was simple: "Help me find You."

God began to reveal Himself in the most unique ways. I encountered generous people everywhere. Each morning as I walked from my big-city apartment to class, complete strangers eagerly inquired whether I needed help crossing the street or directions to my destination. Each time a certain street newspaper salesman saw me out and about, he would say, "Keep straight, girl. Don't give up. You got this." Every meeting felt like a divine whisper of love in which God invited my weary heart to rest, affording me the courage not to give up.

Though I had close friends back home, my touring schedule and life choices had largely disconnected me from my community in Nashville. While in the huge metropolis of New York, where it is easy to get lost in the sea of people and ambition, I was encircled by folks who conveyed God's love. When I confided in one of my new friends my surprise at how intentional people seemed in relationship with others, she simply said, "New York is a big city. People come and go. There is an urgency to go beyond the surface because life is too short to do otherwise"—a lesson I have carried with me since.

Music, which I had intended to avoid while in the city except for weekend concert obligations, also became a pointed display of God's

I am loved by God and others because of who I am, not what I can offer or achieve.

love. The first Sunday after I moved, I visited a small church on Columbia's campus. The next week, I was helping lead worship. And by the end of my New York season, several churches were calling on me to help lead worship, not because I was an artist, but because there was a need. I also had the unique opportunity to provide music for an outreach to homeless folks. Talk about a blessing! Being able to use music, what comes most naturally to me, in these life-giving scenarios, and to use it not just for a personal agenda or ambition but as a gift to others, felt like such a divine expression of love. It seemed God was whispering yet again, *I love you so much that I have given you a gift that reflects my heart. And it's a gift you can give away.* In a city of millions, God's love became personal again.

I LOVE YOU, NOT IN SPITE OF

Andrew: In the first couple years of my recovery process, and even today, nearly a decade later, I still struggle to make decisions based on what I know and want in the thought-through long run versus what I want and feel impulsively in the moment. The world of recovery terms these temporary setbacks as "slips." A slip can be composed of a couple days where I forget who I am and who I want to be and give way to any assortment of behaviors, but it can usually be placed in the past with an emergency counseling session, honest conversations with accountability partners, and a little space to breathe deep and remember that I am loved by God and others because of who I am, not what I can offer or achieve.

Sometimes short-lived slips turn into full-blown relapse. So goes life. Early in my recovery process, I was in Texas visiting my parents. During these times together, my dad and I always try to carve out time for one-on-one conversation. His presence alone encourages an environment where anything can be spoken and is received with no judgment and lots of love. As I began expressing some of my recent poor decisions, the doubts they birthed and the heartache that ensued, Dad listened. Feeling the weight of regret, my emotions surfaced, producing a pesky lump in my throat and blurry eyes.

After my having spoken out loud things that I would never wish to be dumped on any father's head and heart, my dad looked at me directly in my eyes and said, "I love you, son. Not in spite of your stuff, but with all of it."

My dad is awesome. He is certainly human, but a really great human being. If these words were not God displaying His compassionate character through my dad's unconditional love, I give up. I have never felt so valued as a person, just the way I am. I felt as if the shroud of shame protecting my heart from freedom dissipated in one simple sentence, and the heavens began to fill my heart with the truth: *You are okay. You are of value. You are worthy. And you are loved, not in spite of your stuff, but with all of it.*

In a 2013 interview with Tullian Tchividjian, Billy Graham's grandson and pastor of Coral Ridge Presbyterian Church, the new-generation pastor and author quoted Charles Spurgeon to comment on the long-upheld teachings in many churches of performance-based Christianity versus faith through grace, saying, "When I thought God was hard, I found it easy to sin; but when I found God so kind, so good, so overflowing with compassion, I beat my breast to think I could have ever rebelled against One who loved me so and sought my good."[4]

With my tears, layers of shredded garments fell on the banks of Wyoming's Shoshone River in mourning over the losses I had endured throughout my life at the hands of an addiction that defied my place at the table of grace where God says, and has said for all time, that I am worthy—you are worthy—of a place simply because He loves us.

NEVER AGAIN: THE PROMISE AND IN THE DETAILS

READ ISAIAH 54:9-10.

⁹I think this is like the time when Noah lived.
> I promised that I would never again destroy the world
> > by a flood.
> So now I am promising never again to be so angry
> > and punishing as I was when I sent you away.
¹⁰Even if the mountains heave up *from their anchors,*
> and the hills *quiver and* shake, I will not desert you.
> You can rely on My enduring love;
> > My covenant of peace will stand forever.

So says the Eternal One, whose love won't give up on you.

THE PROMISE

Andrew: To keep up with my rent in Nashville while soul-searching out West, I worked for and befriended the owners of a tourist hotel a couple miles outside of Yellowstone National Park's East Entrance. Sitting along the perimeter of the dense Shoshone National Forest, the small mountain resort is centered by William "Buffalo Bill" Cody's hunting lodge, constructed and opened by the distinctive Wild West character in 1904 and utilized to host and entertain famed guests of the American frontier. The icy Shoshone River runs north and south just a few yards east of the old, non-insulated structure. And an early twentieth-century player piano sits flush against the lodge's south wall.

During my first month of work, one of the owners inquired about my background in music. After she learned that I grew up on the piano, she volunteered a key to the old lodge so that the ol' player upright could be at my disposal for whenever my musical whims welled up. Thousands of miles away from home, at the brink of an emotional meltdown and in the middle of a list of spiritual doubts, my most personal occupation—music—was given a house to grow in. What a gift!

My experience with God was now more than scriptural. My faith was now more than the learned traditions of my church upbringing and the testimonies of my parents. Now my relationship with God was personal. As my fingers pressed out new music from those chipped yellow ivories, my heart began to breathe again. And perhaps for the first time, I related to God not only as my Father, or as a redeemed product of His salvation, but as my *friend*.

In Isaiah 54, after years in exile, God vocalizes permanent love for His people for the first time in the Old Testament. Yes, He has shown His love through merciful acts, withholding judgment and restoring order post-judgment, often repeated. But His first out-loud promise of love is found here, directly following chapter 53's prophesy of a Redeemer, a Universal Healer. How perfect.

Feeling spiritually stranded, thousands of miles away from home, I am offered a piano, the instrument on which I first learned music. It was a spiritual lifesaver considering music was the medium that first introduced me to God through songs about Jesus—the channel by which I first heard God's out-loud promise of love to me. How absolutely perfect.

As I probe God's direct promise of unconditional love to the Israelites here, and as I remember the benchmarks of my own personal spiritual journeys, I am convinced that God is in the details.

Ginny: Since I can't see, every day of my life is a testament to God's attention to detail. The insignificant specifics of any given day can foster huge frustrations, especially since I have more important things on my plate than managing the minute details that sighted people can take for granted. Getting a ride to the grocery store or a lift to an important meeting, or making sure I've correctly matched my clothes and removed the stray mascara from my nose before hitting the stage, can prove most challenging. And more often than not, I ask God to literally be in the details.

Several days ago, I was exceptionally frustrated plotting point A to point B. After I prayed a simple prayer, "God I can't figure this out. Please help," a neighbor came to mind. I called her up to see if she was available to help. Not only was she happy to oblige, but the mundane task of running an errand turned into a long overdue catch-up dinner. I do not understand exactly how God works in the details. But because I have seen the evidence of His detailed provision, I ask for His help with everything, both the trivial and significant moments of my journey.

IN THE DETAILS

Andrew: When I was six years old, having already witnessed my deep connection with music, my parents gave me a cassette copy of Sandi Patty's children's record *The Friendship Company* for my listening pleasure. Much to my older brothers' dismay, I wore that sucker out. As an intro to the song "We're in This Thing Together," one of the 'lil narrator guys named Gerbert (leave it to the creators of kids' products to utilize creepy nomenclature), having just been let down by his best buddies, tells Sandi that he feels sad and lonely. She tells him that she, too, has felt sad and lonely, and that it's okay to feel those feelings. Then Sandi says, "You

God loves me. God loves you. With all of our stuff.

know what, Gerbert? There's no one else like you. God loves you so much. And not only does He love you, He thinks you're okay!"

I don't know if my parents, or any other Friendship Company consumer, expected to be given a key to the kingdom through a recording designed for kids, but that dialogue purports a pretty simple truth and some pretty profound theology: God loves me. God loves you. With all of our stuff.

The Israelites have been wandering around, back and forth, lost physically and spiritually. Whether of their own disobedient accord, simple human nature, or sheer emotional weariness, they feel sad and lonely. Abandoned. I understand the feeling. I think you do too. When I crossed over the state line of Wyoming, like the Israelites in the wilderness, I thought, *This is what it feels like to be truly alone.* And, like the Israelites, I wondered if God was truly looking out for my good.

In Wyoming, I ended up writing the songs for my entire first record. That seemingly insignificant independently released project put me on the road performing all over the country for groups of folks who were interested in joining me as I musically traversed my journey to friendship with God. That record birthed more records that eventually led to wider and bigger audiences, collaborations and tours and recordings with some of my musical heroes, and even the genesis for writing this book, as my passion became my full-time profession. In my dark night of the soul, who knew what my great Friend would produce through an antique player piano?

Surrendering to a higher power is tough when the leader seems MIA.

> **When I can't see God, when I can't hear God, when I can't feel God, I remember the benchmarks to believe the promise.**

As the Israelites wallowed around in the desert, offering their surrender, taking it back, then offering it up again, they housed the prophecy of and perpetuated the lineage that would give birth to the Son of the Eternal. In the arid confusion of their reoccurring doubt, who knew what their merciful Shepherd would produce through the wandering history of soul-searchers?

Surrendering to a higher power is tough when the leader seems MIA. The intangibles of faith sure are mysterious—and intangible. When I can't see God, when I can't hear God, when I can't feel God, I remember the benchmarks to believe the promise. As my addiction rages, threatening what I believe and who I am, I sit down at a piano out West. I dip my toes in the snowmelt of the Shoshone. With our ancestors in the search of what has been promised, we wade into the chilly Jordan for a glimpse of the Eternal.

QUESTIONS for Reflection

1. What does it mean that "the One who made you will be your husband" (Isa. 54:5)? How does this promise apply to you personally?

2. When have you felt like the barren woman in Isaiah 54:1–8? When have you felt as though God turned His face away from you? How can you find encouragement and strength from these promises?

3. Imagine yourself outside Noah's ark when the flood waters came. When have the struggles of your life made you feel like someone drowning in that flood? When have you felt a sense of hopelessness and despair?

4. The New King James renders verse 9, "For this is like the waters of Noah to Me." How might this sense of God's control over events offer you hope in the midst of despair?

5. When have you experienced such failure in your life that even your friends gave up on you? When have you been tempted to give up on yourself?

6. What does it mean that God's love "won't give up on you" (v. 10)? What does this mean, in practical terms, during those times when everyone else *does* give up on you?

RESCUE ME

(Words and Music: Andrew Greer)

I've been hurting my brother like there's no other
way to respond
Building up an arsenal of bitter accusations like I need
hate to fight him off
Gonna' need some mercy from completely outside
of me to get along
My forte's not forgiveness, so teach me how You
carried that cross for everyone
*When the tide of pride sweeps me into the deep dark
sea*
Will You set Your sails of love, and come and rescue me?
My heart's been breaking in so many places I can't tell
my friends
Too afraid of judgment then picking up the pieces
that I'll just pretend
Carrying a load about a hundred fold heavier than I
can bear
Lord, You'll have to send an angel and really good
advice if I've got one single prayer
*When the tide of doubt sweeps me into the deep dark
sea*
Will You set Your sails of love, and come and rescue me?
Please don't be afraid to show Your glorious face,
and hold our hands in the dark
We're hoping that Your nearness might be enough
forgiveness for all our many wrongs

When the tide of shame sweeps me into the deep dark
    sea
Will You set Your sails of mercy, and come and rescue
    me?

CHAPTER 4

IF YOU WANT ME TO

> "So take me on the pathway that leads me home to You / And I will walk through the valley if You want me to."
>
> —Ginny Owens and Kyle Matthews, "If You Want Me To"

> "The marvelous richness of human experience would lose something of rewarding joy if there were no limitations to overcome. The hilltop hour would not be half so wonderful if there were no dark valleys to traverse."
>
> —Helen Keller

Ginny: If you had asked me as a kid what I wanted to be when I grew up, I would have told you I was going to sing and write songs. I did both all the time. I would spend hours locked away in my room, performing karaoke before a captive audience of dolls, using tandem cassette recorders to create layers of vocal harmonies and express my love for Jesus and boy-crazy tween angst through every composed lyric and melody.

But if you had asked me in high school or college what I intended to do with my adult life, I would have suggested more practical ideas—perhaps a counselor, a journalist, or a youth pastor. By that point, I had realized that the most important thing in life was to belong, and in order to belong, I would need to choose an "acceptable" career path. Performing music beyond the safe haven of my bedroom was nerve-racking; I rarely pulled it off well. The snickers and giggles of my peers convinced me that no matter how much I loved music, it would never make me acceptable.

Since the day I started school, my mom encouraged me, saying that belonging was not the key to unlock life. "Ginny, God has you here for a purpose," she'd say. "But some days you won't feel like that. And when it feels like Jesus is your only friend, trust Him. You belong to Him."

My parents had been praying for my purpose since before I was born. When they found out they were pregnant with me, they knew there was a good chance that I would inherit the degenerative eye conditions plaguing my father's family history. In the middle of her pregnancy, Mom told the Lord that if she had to choose, she'd rather her child have a heart for Him than sight. Though the choice was not hers to make, this offering of surrender certainly helped prepare her for what was to come.

Several months later, I came into the world a completely healthy baby—except for my eyes. Surgeries could not help my right eye, which hadn't formed properly. I had usable vision in the left, but when I was three, a cryotherapy treatment caused it to hemorrhage and I never saw again. Mom says the experience was so traumatic for me, for six weeks after the treatment I hardly got out of bed.

Because my mom and dad were intentional in their quest to make my childhood as normal as possible, I adjusted quickly to my new life of total darkness. With the use of my other four senses,

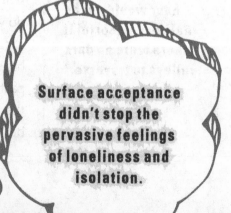

Surface acceptance didn't stop the pervasive feelings of loneliness and isolation.

I became a terribly ordinary kid, climbing the tallest trees, riding my bike, roller-skating down the steepest driveways on our street, and prancing on the balance beam in gymnastics class. When I wasn't being an outdoors daredevil, I was sitting at our dining room piano plunking out the melodies to my favorite songs by ear.

My days of childhood bliss were short-lived. I soon discovered that the greatest challenge of being blind was not the blindness itself, but the reactions of others. Once I started school, my fearless approach to life disappeared as I became aware that because I could not see, I did not belong. And though I've managed to leave behind most of my childhood's awkward moments, one story perfectly sums up my elementary school fate.

In fifth grade, nearly every day during lunch, one of the popular girls in our class entertained the lunchroom by sneaking food off my plate or out of my lunch box. Everyone would giggle, and she would tease loudly, "I stole your food! Why don't you try and find it! Are you scared?" Of course, she wasn't stealing at all. I always knew. I just couldn't figure out how to make her stop.

As I learned the tricks of fitting in, school got easier. I studied hard in order to excel academically. I ran track, made the cheerleading squad, held every office on the Student Council at least once, and never missed a band or choir rehearsal or performance. By the time I graduated, I belonged in many circles. This surface acceptance didn't stop the pervasive feelings of loneliness and isolation, feelings that haunted me into adulthood. I entered college with lots of dreams, and I was certain that realizing those goals would be entirely dependent on my ability to downplay my blindness.

I attended Belmont University in Nashville, Tennessee, where it seemed the vast majority of undergraduates were pursuing the career path of singer-songwriter. While I was still conquering my nerves to get through a performance, my peers had their first records titled and awards acceptance speeches memorized. Though I couldn't bring myself to entirely give up singing, I was still convinced that I'd never be good enough to make it a full-fledged profession.

I also disliked the widely accepted stereotype that every blind person was a musician and felt I had worked too hard to ever settle for that one-dimensional banner. I wanted to prove I was capable of more than singing and playing a piano. My determination led me to pursue dual degrees: commercial vocal performance and music education. At the end of my junior year, in the presence of my peers, one of my professors flippantly remarked that my voice was weak and the odds were slim of my ever making a career of music. That conversation convinced me to drop my performance major, focus my efforts on finishing my education degree, and declare my career path as a high school music teacher. Heading up a choral program would certainly require more skill and tenacity than being a performing singer-songwriter.

After graduation, I began interviewing for teaching positions, only to discover that school administrators were unreceptive to hiring a blind music teacher. My qualifications didn't matter: I graduated with honors and my reference letters spoke highly of my ability to manage a classroom. All they knew was that I could not see. In their eyes, it was impossible to successfully teach when one is blind.

A few months later, I landed a job. I had my own desk, but instead of manning a classroom, I was facilitating meetings for non-profit funding, an aggressive line of work for a non-confrontational, introverted singer-songwriter. I enrolled in graduate school and spent my evenings in class, hoping that a Masters in Music Education would earn me the teaching job I so desperately desired. Life was busy and so empty. The fears and lack of confidence that had trailed me for so many years were now swallowing me whole. I tried to pray for

God's will, but spent most of my time wondering why. Why had He brought me to this dark, desolate place?

GOD CALLING: DESERT ENCOUNTERS AND MOUNTAIN PROMISES

READ EXODUS 3:1–12.

Now *one day* when Moses was shepherding the flock of his father-in-law, Jethro, the priest of Midian, he guided the flock *far away from its usual pastures* to the other side of the desert and came to *a place known as* Horeb, where the mountain of God stood. ²There, the Special Messenger of the Eternal appeared to Moses in a fiery blaze from within the bush. Moses looked again at the bush as it blazed; but *to his amazement*, the bush did not burn up in flames.

Moses *(to himself)*: ³Why is this bush not burning up? I need to move a little closer to *get a better* look at this amazing sight.

⁴When the Eternal One saw Moses approach *the burning bush* to observe it *more closely*, He called out to him from within the bush.

Eternal One: Moses! Moses!

Moses: I'm right here.

Eternal One: ⁵Don't come any closer. Take off your sandals *and stand barefoot on the ground in my presence*, for this ground is holy ground. ⁶I am the True God, *the God* of your father, the God of Abraham, Isaac, and Jacob.

A feeling of dread and awe rushed over Moses; he hid his face because he was afraid he might catch a glimpse of the True God.

Eternal One: ⁷I have seen how My people in Egypt are being mistreated. I have heard their groaning when the slave drivers torment and harass them; for I know well their suffering. ⁸I have come to rescue them from the oppression of the Egyptians, to lead them from that land *where they are slaves and* to give them a good land—a wide, open space flowing with milk and honey. The land is currently inhabited by Canaanites, Hittites, Amorites, Perizzites, Hivites, and Jebusites. [9]The plea of Israel's children has come before Me, and I have observed the cruel treatment they have suffered by Egyptian hands. [10]So go. I'm sending you *back to Egypt as My messenger* to the Pharaoh. *I want you to gather My people*—the children of Israel—and bring them out of Egypt.

Moses *(to God)*: [11]Who am I to confront Pharaoh and lead Israel's children out of Egypt?

Eternal One: [12]*Do not fear, Moses.* I will be with you *every step of the way,* and this will be the sign to you that I am the One who has sent you: after you have led them out of Egypt, you will return to this mountain and worship God.

DESERT ENCOUNTERS

Ginny: Since I was a child, I have known the stories of Moses. As an adult, what moves me most about his journey is how for the first eighty years of his life Moses did not belong.

Moses was born an Israelite in Egypt during a time when Egypt's king was killing all Hebrew boys at birth, yet his mother had hope for her little boy's life and hid him in a woven basket among the reeds on the edge of the Nile River (Ex. 2:2–3). While bathing in the river, an Egyptian princess discovered the Hebrew in hiding and, struck by compassion for the innocent boy, she decided to adopt him, literally saving his life.

Nursed by his biological mother, Moses remained with his Hebrew family for the first few years of his life before moving to the princess's palaces where he was "educated in all the wisdom of the Egyptians" and likely trained in the national military (Acts 7:22 NIV).

With a top-notch education and military expertise, Moses could have found his niche among the young affluence of Pharaoh's court. Instead, he disowned his royal family and returned to the people of his origin to aid in rescuing them from slavery (Acts 7:23–25; Heb. 11:24).

After returning to the Hebrew encampment, he encountered an Egyptian abusing one of his fellow Hebrews and, consumed by anger, he killed the assailant. In an instant of zealous justice, his selfless agenda was shattered. News of the murder spread among the Hebrews and Egyptians, and overnight Moses was rejected by both groups. To save his life, Moses abandoned his homeland, leaving behind all he had ever known, including his dreams of enacting change among his enslaved heritage. He settled in the Midian desert, married the daughter of a priest, and spent the next forty years tending sheep, an up-and-coming liberator confined to the occupation of a shepherd (Ex. 2:12–25).

Exodus 3 opens during one of those humdrum sheep-tending days as Moses watches his father-in-law's flock. Timothy Keller teaches that the Hebrew verb used in verse 1 is a verb of continuance, so the first part of this verse could be translated, "Now Moses was shepherding and shepherding and shepherding the flocks."[1] Scholars disagree on whether Moses was content or miserable as a shepherd, but I can't help thinking that the monotony of caring for sheep day in and day out had to become tedious, especially for someone with the refined skill sets and upper-echelon education of Moses.

Perhaps out of boredom, Moses led the sheep down a detour, ending up at the mountain of God. Here, where there is absolutely nothing else to distract him, he notices and marvels at the bush that is on fire but does not burn up. As he inspects the bush, the Eternal immediately engages him in a life-altering conversation. God calls Moses by name. And then, as if a voice originating from thin air weren't clear enough, God introduces Himself (vv. 3–6).

As the authorship of Exodus is attributed to Moses by most scholars, I take this as a firsthand account of his emotional reaction to encountering his Creator. With "dread and awe" he hides his face to avoid seeing the God of the universe with his limited sight (v. 6). The Eternal's infiniteness is too much to comprehend with human sense. For forty years, this simple shepherd's life has been isolated and dull. He probably assumed that the remainder of his life would be spent in a similar droning rhythm. And suddenly, without notice or opportunity to prepare, he is singled out by God. He must have wondered, *Why?* Or was he too overwhelmed by the power and presence of a first-name basis God to even think, much less consider questioning?

After spending my undergraduate years preparing to teach, I was surprised and dreadfully disappointed to be forced down a detour from my intended occupation. I felt frustrated in the corporate mundanity of my post-college desert. As I fulfilled my daily routine of work and graduate school, I wondered if I would ever feel hopeful or enthusiastic again or if this was just part of ordinary life—possibly indefinitely. I wondered where God was. I couldn't hear His voice above the noise of my questions. I couldn't find His peace in the moments when I felt most isolated and alone. Did He care? Had He led me here on purpose, or had I taken a wrong turn, resulting in an unproductive consequence?

But gradually, with no distractions of achievement or self-motivated success, I began to truly discover God. Through my solitude, His whispers invited me to come closer.

Though I had professed my faith in Him since age four, in the core of my heart, I believed that He saw me the way the rest of the world did: as slightly less usable. I never considered that He would save me for a specific purpose with tangible impact. But the eventual surrender of my desert experience created a spiritual oasis where the Eternal could truly reveal Himself to me. I was amazed by God in a way I had never experienced before. I grew more willing, even eager, to wait and listen and be mindful of whom I was waiting and listening for. As the God of the universe was preparing me for my involvement in His bigger story, I was compelled to worship Him with a new gratefulness for His presence in our lives.

On a side note, I am acutely aware of how many people endure desert seasons for years, sometimes an entire lifetime. I have received thousands of letters and emails from folks, especially those with disabilities, who feel that God has left them for dead in the desert. As we continue to explore Moses' season of seeming purposelessness, my hope is that all of our perspectives will be widened and our hearts encouraged to outlast even the longest and darkest of midnights.

MOUNTAIN PROMISES

Ginny: As the Eternal continues dialoguing with Moses, He issues the plan for delivering the Israelites from slavery—and that plan will be carried out by Moses. He has heard their groaning, knows their suffering well, and is eager not simply to rescue them, but to give them the fruitful land which He promised to Moses' forefather Abraham (Gen. 17:8; Ex. 3:7–9).

This desire to remove the Israelites from their current oppressive circumstances—and to then deliver them into flourishing

> **God understands pain and is completely faithful in the middle of the ache.**

circumstances—affirms that God understands pain and is completely faithful in the middle of the ache. Because Moses knows the misery of the Hebrews firsthand, I am sure he is overwhelmed, perhaps even to the point of disbelief, to hear that the Eternal is finally going to intervene. But I cannot imagine the shock and horror that must have ensued in Moses' heart and mind when he received what the Lord said to him next: "So go" (Ex. 3:10).

Through this simple, direct call, God is leading Moses to the foot of a proverbial mountain, which Moses is scared of and unable to comprehend how to climb. Moses responds by barraging God with his doubts and questions of "how," yet God, in His brilliant creativity, has been preparing Moses to undertake this initiative his entire life. He is a Hebrew who has always desired to see his people freed. He is an Egyptian with the practical skills to interact with the king. And most importantly, his life experience has humbled him to the point where he would never attempt such a grandiose task without strength and guidance from the Eternal.

He conveys his doubts to God with the famous "Who am I?" quandary (v. 11). In other words: "Are You kidding me? God, do You remember how I had to escape Egypt in order to live? Are You aware that the Egyptians and Hebrews both hate me? Do You know that I am old?"

God's answer is not a reply to Moses' pity party, but a word of spiritual assurance: "Do not fear, Moses. I will be with you every step of the way" (v. 12). God does not affirm Moses' qualifications or lack thereof. He simply guarantees His presence along the way. As God led me from the

> **God does not affirm Moses' qualifications or lack thereof. He simply guarantees His presence along the way.**

desert to the foot of my own life mountain, my confidence came in discovering God's qualifications, His knowledge and power, not my own. *Ginny, do not fear. I will be with you every step of the way.*

"And this will be the sign to you that I am the One who has sent you: after you have led them out of Egypt, you will return to this mountain and worship God" (v. 12). For me, the second part of verse 12 has become one of the most significant moments of God's encounter with Moses. After the Eternal successfully rescues the Hebrews from Egypt (through Moses), they spend nearly a year on this mountain. On the first day of that year, Moses strikes a rock that gushes water for the thirsting people and livestock who have not had drinking water in weeks (Ex. 17:6). He later receives the dramatic Ten Commandments transmission (Ex. 31:18), as well as step-by-step instructions on the tabernacle to be constructed on this mountain site (Ex. 25–30). And the first Passover since the exodus from Egypt is celebrated here (Num. 9:1–5).

God's mountain is beautiful and complex. It contains the calling that looms before us and seems unconquerable, yet as we rely on and rest in His strength, the mountain becomes a home for Him to love and nurture us in. And after the strain and stress and trial of the climb, the mountain transforms into a benchmark of perspective where we return to worship God, remembering how He accomplished His promise and purpose in our lives.

When I reflect on the season of doubt and confusion preceding my music career, I can barely comprehend how God used that period of time to prepare me for the mountain of career I was about to climb. During that season of drought, I wrote songs that would unexpectedly encourage others facing their own deserts. The capacity to trust in God through every circumstance grew, a trust I would exercise over and over again in the treacherous life still to come. And as I think on Him, His faithfulness then and now, I return to worship.

GOD IN THE DETAILS: *MY NAME IS* AND THE BIG PICTURE INVITATION

READ EXODUS 3:13–22.

Moses: [13]Let's say I go to the people of Israel and tell them, "The God of your fathers has sent me to *rescue* you," and then they reply, "What is His name?" What should I tell them then?

Eternal One: [14]I AM WHO I AM. This is what you should tell the people of Israel: "I AM has sent me to *rescue* you."

[15]This is what you are to tell Israel's people: "The Eternal, the God of your fathers, the God of Abraham, the God of Isaac, and the God of Jacob is the One who has sent me to you." This is My name forevermore, and this is the name by which all future generations shall remember Me.

[16]Round up all the elders in Israel and tell them, "The Eternal, the God of your fathers and the God of Abraham, Isaac, and Jacob, has revealed Himself to me and said, 'I have been watching over you, and I am *deeply* troubled by what has been done to you in Egypt. [17]So I will rescue you from the oppression you have suffered in Egypt, and lead you to the land of the Canaanites, Hittites, Amorites, Perizzites, Hivites, and Jebusites—a *rich and productive* land flowing with milk and honey.'?" [18]They will listen to all that you tell them; you and the elders will then go to visit Egypt's king and tell the king, "The Eternal, the Hebrews' God, has appeared to us. We ask that you allow us to travel three days' distance into the desert to offer sacrifices to the Eternal."

[19]But I *already* know that Egypt's king *will turn down your request. He* will not allow you to go, unless he is compelled by a hand stronger than his own. [20]So I will stretch out My hand, *display*

My power, and crush Egypt with a series of miracles I will perform. After that the king will send you out *of Egypt.* [21]I will make it so the Egyptians treat *My* people favorably; and when you leave *Egypt,* you will not leave empty-handed. [22]Every *Hebrew* woman will ask her *Egyptian* neighbor and any foreigner in her home for anything made of silver or gold or even *fine* clothing. You will give all the items you collect to your children to wear. In this way, you will strip these items from the Egyptians.

MY NAME IS

Ginny: Moses asks God a strange question. Essentially he says, "Who should I tell the Israelites You are?" (v. 13). This seemingly basic but fair inquiry leads me to wonder what the Israelites think or know of God at this point. Living in the Egyptian's polytheistic society without a conscientious spiritual leader to remind them of the Eternal or speak His words to them, perhaps they have honestly forgotten who He is. Debilitated from hundreds upon hundreds of years of national enslavement, maybe they wonder if He even exists. I know I would be tempted to think like that.

God doesn't seem deterred in the least by Moses' foundational question. Quite the opposite. For the first time, God unveils His name, a description far more intricate and complex than the supreme "god" characteristics He has been labeled by thus far in Scripture. I AM WHO I AM. By revealing His personal signature, God is digging in deep with the Israelites. He is now more than a supreme judge, some guide in the sky or a universal creator. Through His name's meaning, God is now identifying with His people directly, telling Moses that He is "The LORD [Yahweh] God of your fathers, the God of Abraham, the God of Isaac, and the God of Jacob" (v. 15 NKJV). Furthermore, this Eternal "I AM" is not merely some detached being who is not involved in the affairs of His people; rather, He is deliberately sending Moses to intervene in those affairs.

As John Piper states, nomenclature is important because "in Scripture, a person's name often signifies his character or ability or mission, especially when the name is given by God."[2] God changes Abram's name to "Abraham" when He dubs him the father of many nations (Gen. 17:5). In Hebrew, Abraham means "father of a multitude." In Genesis 32, God renames Jacob "Israel" as a blessing for prevailing in his struggle with God. How appropriate. Many scholars believe "Israel" means "Let God rule."[3] And now, by revealing His true name, God reveals who He truly is. More than a looming omniscient, omnipotent deity, He is a God with feelings for His people. And out of His connected concern, He is writing an intimate—and breathtaking—story of deliverance (vv. 16–17).

The Hebrew word translated "I AM" in these verses is a simple word meaning "to be," comparable to our English word *is*. God spoke this word when He created the universe, saying "Let there *be* light" (Gen. 1:3, emphasis added), in effect speaking His very nature into the universe itself. Jesus used the same construction when the Pharisees asked Him who He is, identifying Himself with the Father: "Very truly I tell you . . . before Abraham was born, I am!" (John 8:58 NIV).

The all-powerful presence who made a covenant with Abraham, wrestled with Jacob, called Moses to rescue His people, and invaded history by relating to us in human form to restore the relationship with Him that was broken by sin is the same God who is giving us confidence to meet our often challenging purposes head on by naming us worthy of the call. This personal engagement that Yahweh is initiating in our day-to-day lives makes responding to His prompt, His

The author of the big, overall story is inviting me to trust Him in my individual story.

call, unavoidable. The author of the big, overall story is inviting me to trust Him in my individual story, an infinitely more intimate role than the impersonal edicts of some disengaged deity.

THE BIG PICTURE INVITATION

Ginny: As an out of work music educator, I could never have imagined what God was establishing for me and my career. In the middle of a series of slammed doors, one small opportunity that I never would have expected was extended to me, and it opened up a world of possibilities for my future in music.

Several months after playing a song in church that I had written, I ended up in an interview with a music publisher. As I entered his office, I internally analyzed if I should have warned him that I couldn't see in order to avoid another awkward situation. The anxiety was unwarranted. I played him my songs, he liked them, and a few months later he signed me to his publishing company. Within a year, he had helped me land a record deal.

This was not the path I had planned, and every affirmation was a complete surprise. I often felt like the dream I had been afraid to embrace was finally coming true. Yet I was apprehensive about all the mountain climbing that this new direction entailed. I, too, had met I AM in the desert. And what I learned from getting to know Him during the dry season gave me courage to forge ahead in the fertile adventure unfolding. I had complete confidence that He would orchestrate my entire story, including my developing career as a recording artist. And most importantly, I was understanding that my story was a living, breathing part of His bigger story.

Andrew: Unlike Ginny, who was commencing what has become an illustrious singer-songwriter career, I was beginning a not-so-distinguished course when I enrolled as a music major at Belmont University in the early 2000s—or among professionals working in the music industry after graduation. The small town I had grown up in had supported my musical talents well, affording me gracious platforms to learn, grow, and showcase what I was musically capable of at the time. And because music was such a big part of how I expressed my spirituality, I assumed that anywhere I went the world would provide space to facilitate it.

Once I hit the pavement at Belmont, I quickly learned that I was a guppy in a sea of sharks. And these peer musicians were big fish for a reason; they were *that* good. Though I was coolly accepted in my commercial piano program, I wondered if I would find more applause as a vocal major. At the end of my freshman year, having received encouragement from certain advisors in and outside of the school of music, I auditioned to swap majors. The audition went well, I thought. But when I was notified that I had not been accepted as a commercial voice major, my pride was hurt and my brain was confused. This road had been recommended by those who were now saying, "Sorry, Charlie." I didn't understand the seemingly two-faced rejection.

Dr. Emily Bullock, an incredible mezzo-soprano and integral member of Belmont's classical voice faculty at the time, had been in my audition for the mandatory classical selections. After she heard about the commercial major denial, she reached out to let me know that she loved my voice, and I would have a welcome home in the classical voice department if I was interested. Though I had no intention or desire to become an opera star, I did appreciate the classics and realized

When the Eternal calls, He wants us to rely on Him to get the job done.

that this might be a viable option for completing my music degree while expanding my vocal chops.

Fast forward ten years, and I am using my voice on the road in tough scenarios—long days on the road, hard nights performing, and wide-ranging vocal utility during concerts. Had it not been for Dr. Bullock's super attention and traditional training, I would have certainly damaged my voice and been significantly more limited in the ways I now use it and control it, devastating scenarios for a touring artist. Even more significant, as a singer-songwriter, I am interested in going beyond the connection from onstage perfor- mance to connecting with people and expressing the love of Jesus before, during, and after a show. My classical diversion fitted me with the practical resources to stay healthy so I can keep the small-picture reality of performing alive, assisting the bigger-picture desire to serve God by serving people through music.

This is not the story of a traumatic tragedy or disease, but in my heart it required a complete priority rearrangement to under- stand the audition's outcome and what that implied for my future at school, and possibly in music. As my heart relaxed after the initial hurt and my mind began to broaden in processing the next practical steps, I, like Ginny, plowed through my walls of fear with a sense of surrender to God's bigger story.

Ginny: God gives Moses the fortitude of perspective so he can feel confident to initiate the Israelites' move from slavery to the promised land. God knows what is to come. He understands the storms that are brewing as an obstacle to the Israelites' freedom, and so He gives Moses a taste of the reception he will receive as he transmits I AM's message. Israel's elders will heed his leadership; Pha- raoh will not (vv. 18–19). Insight into the immediate future further confirms that the Eternal is truly the one conversing with Moses through this mysterious exchange.

He also gives Moses the authority to speak in the name of God (v. 16). Though many men have used the "authority of God" to manipulate people into cultish discipleship, this true God encounter reminds me that when the Eternal calls, He wants us to rely on Him to get the job done. This is good news!

The events that follow create one of the most famous and celebrated dramas in the history of man—horrid plagues, miraculous transformations, creation-defying signs and wonders. The Eternal knows that disciples will remember this benchmark of faith until the end of time. Psalms will be inspired by the journey. The Jews will cling tightly to this promise during their extended exile. And we will discuss it, meditate on it, and write songs about it more than three thousand years later. But in that moment, Moses could never have imagined the magnitude of the story he would help perpetuate.

The same is true for me. I will never fully understand the role I play in God's bigger story. And so I am inspired to live pursuing what God wants in every moment.

EMBRACING GOD'S BIGGER STORY: BABY STEPS AND STRENGTHS IN WEAKNESS

READ EXODUS 4:1–12.

Moses: What if they don't trust me? What if they don't listen to a single word I say? They are *more likely* to reply: "The Eternal has not revealed Himself to you."

The Eternal One answered Moses.

Eternal One: [2]What do you have in your hand?

Moses: My *shepherd's* staff.

Eternal One: [3]Throw your staff down on the ground.

So Moses threw the staff on the ground, and it was transformed into a snake. Moses quickly jumped back *in fear.*

Eternal One: [4]Reach out and grab it by the tail.

Despite his natural fears, Moses reached out and grabbed the snake; and as he held it, it changed back into a shepherd's staff.

Eternal One: [5]This *sign* is so the people will believe that I, the God of their fathers—Abraham, Isaac, and Jacob—have revealed Himself to you.
[6]Now *for the second sign.* Put your hand *on your chest* inside your shirt.

Moses did as the Eternal instructed; and when he pulled his hand out, his hand was covered with some disease *that made it look* as white as snow.

Eternal One: [7]Put your hand back inside your clothes.

Moses again did as He instructed, and when he removed his hand from his shirt, it returned *to normal* like the rest of his skin.

Eternal One: [8-9]If they refuse to believe you, and are not persuaded after *you perform* the first sign, perhaps they will be after the second sign. But if they refuse to believe you and are not persuaded after *you perform* the first two signs, then *here is a third sign:* Take some water from the Nile and pour it out onto the ground. The water you take from the Nile will become blood on the ground.

Moses: [10]Please, Lord, *I am not a talented speaker.* I have never been good with words. I wasn't when I was younger and I haven't gotten any better since You revealed Yourself to me. I stutter and stammer. My words get all twisted.

Eternal One: [11]Who is it that gives a person a mouth? Who determines whether one person speaks and another doesn't? Why is it that one person hears and another doesn't? And why can one person see and another doesn't? Isn't it *because of* Me, the Eternal? *You know it is.* [12]Go now, and I will be there to give you the words to speak; I will tell you what to say.

BABY STEPS

Ginny: The Eternal has engaged Moses in detailed conversation and foretold the future as evidence that He knows, He sees, and He cares for the Hebrew people. Shouldn't this be enough to inspire trust? Yet the cautious shepherd remains doubtful and full of questions. He anticipates persistent rejection from his fellow Israelites, stacking up a list of "what ifs" for God to answer before he acts (v. 1). How very human of Moses.

When God introduced Himself to me anew in my post-college professional wilderness, I also had doubts and questions about my future. *What if being blind gets in the way of every possible great opportunity? What if You are not enough to carry me into a more hopeful season?* Even at the foot of the mountain of my calling and dream, I doubted. *God, what if I am not a good enough singer or songwriter to pull this off?* I shudder to think how often my own list of "what ifs" has kept me from taking the next step in trust.

God responds to Moses' question with a question of His own. "What do you have in your hand?" (v. 2). What an inspiring question. I hear this question as, *What have I given you to work with?* What unknowable power and ability do we possess in the gifts and talents, great and small, given to us by the Eternal?

Moses is holding a shepherd's staff, a rather innocuous tool. But this is all the resource he will need to persuade the Israelites that I AM is at work. God will use Moses' simple staff for countless miracles in the coming years, including the Egyptian plagues, walling up the Red Sea, and extracting enough water from a rock to satiate the thirst of six hundred thousand thirsty Hebrews in the desert.

The Eternal transforms Moses' staff into a snake, naturally initiating a panic attack in Moses. But God commands him to grab the snake's tail, returning the staff to its original lifeless form, and Moses complies. Here it seems Moses' one small act of obedience strengthens his faith in the Eternal, even if slightly. Then God asks him to remove his hand from his shirt to find that it is infected with a leprous disease as the Eternal's second sign of proof, and there is no comment of anxiety in Moses. Instead, he follows God's commands to a tee, places it back inside his shirt, and removes it completely healed (vv. 3–7). These are just baby steps to belief.

The remainder of Moses' life involves moments just like these. God instructs, Moses trusts, then he obeys. Through every exercise, Moses' faith in the Eternal strengthens, and the relationship that grows with the Eternal testifies to the beauty of surrender.

In my life, learning to trust means taking baby steps of faith. Trust means walking through each dark moment with the knowledge that God is with me, even when I don't feel His presence. As I continue living, God reveals evidence of Himself in daily details. And as I recognize that evidence, my faith in my ability is replaced by faith in God's capabilities. Today, I am grateful that I can place every aspect of my life into His strong, capable hands.

STRENGTH IN WEAKNESS

Ginny: God arms Moses for his immediate journey, but he still feels weak and ill equipped. Perhaps he is terrified of abandoning his comfortable, albeit dreadfully boring, shepherd's existence for the radical potential of God's liberating appointment. Once his practical doubts are quelled, his excuses kick in: "Please, Lord, *I am not a talented speaker . . .* I stutter and stammer. My words get all twisted" (v. 10).

I can relate to his hesitation. Somehow, it is always about me. My fears of the unknown, my doubts, my flaws all must be more limiting than the Eternal's competence.

Andrew: Like Moses, like Ginny, I struggle to surrender. I suppose the reluctance to let go is one common denominator of humanity. And the inability to lay it down, hand it over, surrender is indicative of the finite's doubt of the infinite.

Though doubt plays such an eager role in my understanding of and lack of surrender to God and the spiritual realm, spending my formative years in a household that facilitated open conversation, encouraging rather than squelching questions born of doubt—questions that asked God to reveal Himself—surrender was deeply entrenched in the questioning. By asking, *Where are You God?* I was acknowledging an innate belief in His existence. Though I couldn't detect His purpose or practical role in every circumstance, faith was formulating questions on my lips and producing surrender, bit by bit, in my heart. In my experience with the bigger eternal picture, doubt establishes, rather than diminishes, my faith.

Ginny: I continue to learn that surrender to God is as much about relying on His strength as it is about owning up to my weaknesses. The dry spell I experienced after college initiated this perspective shift from what I have to offer to what God can do. I had spent years working hard to be self-reliant so people would see past my blindness. I refused to consider that my lack of sight might be a God-purposed part of me.

Blindness was a sign of brokenness. Who wants to wear brokenness as a badge for all to notice? Who wants to allow her weakness to be on display? Give me a few more years of life experience, and I am convinced that the weak, broken parts of me have the most potential to encourage and relate to others in the ways the put-together me simply cannot.

As if God were unaware, Moses tells God of his own weakness. He confesses that his speech gets all jumbled. He stutters. His articulation is unclear. Whether this is a last ditch effort to avoid God's plan or a deep-seated insecurity, God doesn't dismiss Moses from the task He has in mind: "Who is it that gives a person a mouth? Who determines whether one person speaks and another doesn't? Why is it that one person hears and another doesn't? And why can one person see and another doesn't? Isn't it *because of* Me, the Eternal? *You know it is*" (v. 11).

I find this dialogue freeing and thought-provoking. The great I AM, the Eternal, my heavenly Father, gives me His power and strength in the middle of my weakness. Countless passages of Scripture tell us of God's affinity for the weak. As God would tell the apostle Paul more than a thousand years later, "My power is made perfect in weakness" (2 Cor. 12:9). Since the beginning of time, God has used persons perceived as weak to work His miracles.

God hears Moses' fear. He acknowledges his insecurities. And He expresses once more His call to the eighty-year-old shepherd, this time with a follow-up of assurance: "Go now, and I will be there to give you the words to speak; I will tell you what to say" (v. 12). In the middle of Moses' circumstances, in the reality of my blindness, and in the center of your challenges, He equips us with unique gifts, supported by His strength to use

> **Since the beginning of time, God has used persons perceived as weak to work His miracles.**

them effectively every time, and calls us to go. Surrender. Leave the ordinary behind and embrace the extraordinary story that only the Eternal could author.

WHEN GOD CALLS

Ginny: Though God may not outline His tasks as blatantly for us today, we can relate to aspects of His Old Testament callings. What can we learn about surrender, faith, and trust when facing the mountain in front of us? Here is a short list of Old Testament calls that require faith, surrender, and trust to act on.

> **Genesis 12:1–4:** God's call to Abram is outrageous, but he obeys without question.
>
> **1 Samuel 3:1–10:** God calls the boy priest to greater things than he could ever imagine.
>
> **Hosea 1:1–11:** Hosea receives a unique call during a particularly rebellious season in Israelite history.
>
> **Jonah 1–4:** God calls the prophet Jonah to love people whom he simply doesn't like.

QUESTIONS for Reflection

1. Suppose that you were an ordinary shepherd (disregarding Moses' background) and you spotted a bush that was on fire—but not burning up. What would you do? How would you react if God's voice suddenly called you by name?

2. Consider the traits of God's character that Exodus 3 reveals. How do those traits relate to your life at present? Spend some time in worship, reflecting on God's character and praising Him for it.

3. Imagine yourself in Moses' place, experiencing the dramatic signs of the serpent-rod and "some disease" on your hand (some translations suggest leprosy). How would you have reacted? What would you have said to God?

4. Given your response to those miraculous signs, would you have responded to God's call as Moses did (v. 10)? Why or why not? If not, what excuses would *you* have offered?

5. What weaknesses or inadequacies in your life do you feel are keeping you from a more effective or vibrant relationship with God?

6. Given God's response to Moses' excuse (v. 11), how might He respond concerning *your* weaknesses?

IF YOU WANT ME TO

(Words and Music: Ginny Owens / Kyle Matthews)

The pathway is broken and the signs are unclear
And I don't know the reasons why You brought me
    here.
But just because You love me the way that You do
I'm gonna walk through the valley if You want me to.
No, I'm not who I was when I took my first step
And I'm clinging to the promise You're not through
    with me yet.
So if all of these trials bring me closer to You
Then I will walk through the fire if You want me to.
It may not be the way I would've chosen
When You lead me through a world that's not my
    home
But You never said it would be easy
You only said I'd never go alone.
So when the whole world turns against me, and I'm
    all by myself
And I can't hear You answer my cries for help
I'll remember the suffering Your love put You
    through
And I will walk through the darkness if You want me
    to.
And when I cross over Jordan
I'm gonna sing and I'm gonna shout
I'm gonna look into Your eyes and see

You never let me down

So take me on the pathway that leads me home to
   You

And I will walk through the valley if You want me to.

If You Want Me To
Written by Kyle Matthews and Ginny Owens
Copyright © 1999 Universal Music - Brentwood Benson Publ.
(ASCAP) (adm. at CapitolCMGPublishing.com) All rights reserved.
Used by permission.

CHAPTER 5

MINE EYES (LOOK TO THE HILLS)

"He gave us bones / He gave us blood / He gave us heart to feel everything / I felt the break / I stopped the pulse / Prayed it away still no relief..."

—Andrew Greer and Emily DeLoach, "Mine Eyes"

"Magnanimous Despair alone / Could show me so divine a thing, / Where feeble Hope could ne'er have flown, / But vainly flapped its tinsel wing."

—Andrew Marvell, "The Definition of Love"

"Be kind, for everyone you meet is fighting a hard battle."

—Anonymous, attributed to twentieth-century theologian Ian McLaren

Andrew: The year was 1992. I was nine years old, and my mother had masterfully prepared for our family of five to head east for a spring break getaway in Florida. More specifically, we were going to Disney World. And most exciting, we were making the 1,200-mile trek by airplane from Dallas-Fort Worth's musty metroplex to the land where dreams come true. For a fourth grader, I was living the high life.

Part of our magical itinerary included a jaunt to Charlotte Sports Park in Port Charlotte, Florida, to attend a Texas Rangers spring training game. My older brother Chris and I were avid Major League Baseball fans with affinities for Topps collectible cards, the Rangers, and Rafael Palmeiro—the Lone Star franchise's first baseman and designated hitter, a young All-Star thanks to his defensive infield skills and blooming batting average. Chris and I cheered Palmeiro closely, and we were ecstatic to witness Palmeiro's superhuman abilities in person.

Nine innings felt like nine minutes, and soon the post-game ruckus began. Eager fans—us included—swarmed the steep concrete steps lining the outside of the players' locker room for a once-in-a-lifetime high-five or autograph from any player brave enough to stick his neck out into the beehive of baseball disciples. Chris and I were not too proud, and we wanted to participate in the collectors' lottery. So armed with Palmeiro paraphernalia, we squeezed our preteen frames to the top of the stairs.

In what seemed like slow-motion destiny, the Gold Glove great leaned out a second story window to gift his John Hancock to the highest reacher. Being four years my senior and a head taller than me (still true in our thirties), Chris could easily reach the Palmeiro in-demand digits. The Holy Grail. But no matter how hard I tried to push and shove, my burgeoning towhead couldn't quite cap the crowd.

Chris is the middle child. Where my oldest brother Trey assumed the firstborn position of leader with great ease, Chris embodied some of the invisible tendencies of the in-between sibling. Because of Mom and Dad's relaxed, attentive

> Because we are separated from God, we desire things that He in His infinite wisdom is not willing to prescribe.

parenting style, rarely did any of us feel forgotten. Trey talked nonstop, a sometimes endearing quality, and I asserted my unsolicited opinion frequently enough with sarcasm and bite, qualities always exercised but never fully appreciated. But Chris was always a bit more mysterious. He was more prone to listen, to observe or ignore, or to go back to his room and crank up early-90s Garth Brooks. Don't judge; you did too.

Chris is also one of the most tender and compassionate people I know. But, like any good brother, he could be merciless. An example? After I was dismissed from junior high for a week as an extreme case of poison ivy healed (and in order to keep from traumatizing peers with my leprous appearance) Chris nicknamed me "Magnum P.I."—as in "Poison Ivy." How sweet. A few years earlier, against my mother's warning, he yelled, "Four eyes!" the instant I sheepishly exited our family van after getting my first pair of glasses. Talk about getting hit while you are already down. But when not harassing, Chris was—and always has been—a protector and source of emotional affirmation. He is a consistent companion as I look out, act on, and think about the many confusions of my life.

And on that sunny spring training day, he quietly slipped his prized Palmeiro Topps card in his pocket, swiped my flimsy Donruss collector's card from my tight clinch, and stretched up just in time for *the* Rafael Palmeiro to imprint his Sharpie across *my* card and hand it back to Chris. I still treasure that card.

Fast forward twenty years. Chris was engaged to a beautiful woman named Kerry. Because Chris's nature is generally kind and hospitable, he can be an easy target for relationship manipulation, where his significant other uses his best traits to guilt him into staying when the partnership simply is not healthy. Kerry, however, supported and loved my brother with a natural ease that enhanced rather than diminished Chris's finer attributes. I was thrilled for my brother.

Late in their engagement, Chris began to feel anxiety about the pending nuptials. Though his love and desire for Kerry had not changed, there was growing discomfort developing around the wedding date. Being a thirty-something bachelor, Chris chalked up his fears to cold feet. But he couldn't shake the notion that what he was feeling was deeper than a surface scare, that perhaps there was deeper meaning stirring the currents of his heart.

Through private counseling and unyielding self-analysis, Chris decided it would be best to postpone his and Kerry's wedding until he could get a better handle on the doubts plaguing his heart and mind. Kerry adamantly disagreed with Chris's decision to wait, and she did not understand the rationale behind the postponement. Chris didn't completely understand it himself. The morning after he called off the ceremony, Chris lost his job. What began as a difficult decision about a marriage date, turned into a comprehensive living nightmare.

Under the strain and stress of so many changing tides, the engagement completely ended. Through hours-long nighttime conversations, I witnessed my brother's midnight pains. Chris was experiencing the most poignant mental, emotional, and spiritual conflict of his life. One moment he was resigned to the idea that God was indeed in control and all would work out for his good (Rom. 8:28). The next minute he was, quite literally, cursing his Creator for instigating the doubt that caused the divide between him and his beloved, who herself was now experiencing an onslaught of old and new personal conflicts from the decision aftermath.

In those very human moments, real life happened—not just in Chris's immediate and very potent heart-aching circumstances, but in the mysterious and often hard to understand bigger-picture spiritual realm where heaven and earth collide.

THE TRUTH: DISCERNING FALSE PROPHETS AND OPEN YOUR EARS, SHUT YOUR MOUTH

READ ISAIAH 36:1–10.

After Hezekiah had been *Judah's* king for 14 years, King Sennacherib of Assyria launched an attack against Judah's fortified cities and conquered them. ²Sennacherib sent *his right-hand man (whom they call the Rabshakeh)* to King Hezekiah in Jerusalem along with an army *to intimidate him.* The Rabshakeh came from Lachish, *formerly a great Judean city,* and stationed himself along the highway that skirts the field where they launder the cloth, near the aqueduct for the upper pool. ³Three men *from Hezekiah's court* came down *from the palace* to meet him there. They were Hilkiah's son Eliakim, the palace administrator; Shebna, the royal secretary; and Asaph's son Joah, the recorder.

⁴The Rabshakeh told them to relay to Hezekiah these words of *Sennacherib,* the great king of Assyria.

Rabshakeh: How come you're so sure of yourself? ⁵Your strategy and strength for war seem to be limited to *diplomacy and* empty words. Now that you have rebelled against me, who are you really relying on? ⁶Take a look! Are you really counting on the help of a crushed reed, Egypt, *against me?* Relying on Egypt is like leaning on a splintering stick that ends up jabbing you through the palm. That's the way Pharaoh, king of Egypt, is to everyone who relies on him. ⁷Or maybe you'll tell me, "We are putting our trust in the Eternal One our God." *Hah! I don't think so.* Don't forget that Hezekiah went around destroying all His altars and wrecking His places of worship, insisting that Judah and Jerusalem must worship before the one altar *in Jerusalem.*

⁸Come on now. Make a deal with my master, the king of Assyria: I'll give you 2,000 horses if you can do your part and deliver the same number of riders. ⁹How can you repel even the weakest unit in

my master's army when you have to look to Egypt for chariots and drivers? ¹⁰And just in case you think that I'm attacking you of my own volition, *you should know that I am not.* Your God, the Eternal, sent me. Your God said to me, "Rise up against that land *(namely you Judeans)*, and destroy it."

DISCERNING FALSE PROPHETS

Andrew: (A side note: because of Isaiah's personal prophetic dialogue with Judah during this Assyrian-Jerusalem drama, the book of Isaiah contains the most comprehensive account of this story. Two abbreviated accounts with minor nuances occur in 2 Kings 18 and 2 Chronicles 32.)

As evidenced throughout history, the Middle East is no stranger to territorial conflict. When Judah is attacked by Assyria under Hezekiah's reign in 701 BC, the Northern Kingdom (Israel) is already under Assyrian control, and the crusading nation's importation of people throughout the Eastern world has distilled Israelite religious influence—causing dissent from the people of Judah, who are experiencing economic, political, and spiritual stability at the time. As in any human crusade, more power leads to more conquests, and Sennacherib, Assyria's king, is currently taking names, with his sights set on his archrival's spiritual epicenter: Jerusalem.

Though you may be rolling your eyes at another summary of a biblical battle, Hezekiah's challenge is an opportunity to understand how scriptural history reiterates the notion that God does not operate tit for tat. The dictatorial,

God's sovereignty relies solely on His character.

micromanaging personality often prescribed to the God of the Old Testament by generations of believers who have been scarred by legalistic pasts is simply not present in this passage. Instead, God's sovereignty, His authority or prerogative as Creator of the cosmos, relies solely on His character. God is operating out of His innate qualities, which we are trying to carefully uncover throughout this book.

God's people are being attacked by their neighbors once again, just as they were in the time of Jehoshaphat (see chapter 1). New century, same story. Judah, though in a season of spiritual health, is not immune to the greed of its neighbors. In fact, the first tangible threat is prescribed by Sennacherib's hatchet man, the Rabshakeh, a man of Judean descent, shrewdly selected to deliver a twisted tale to his own people in Judah. In verse 7, the Rabshakeh accuses the highly regarded Hezekiah of demolishing God's places of worship—a reference to Hezekiah's elimination of the bronze serpent that Moses had made after it became a tool for idolatrous worship in 2 Kings 18:4—in order to discount Hezekiah's spiritual leadership. Then he claims Sennacherib's determination to destroy Judah as a direct order from God (v. 10).

Fact: the Israelites had begun to immortalize and worship artifacts from the Jewish journey as gods, rather than utilize them as a sacred reminder of the God who had consistently and intimately delivered them from their harried past. Hezekiah's sacred purge was not unlike many modern-day Christians' attempts to prioritize relationship with God over worship of highly regarded monuments of the faith, such as statues of celebrated saints traditionally found in liturgical houses of worship.

Hezekiah has acted with spiritual integrity. But the Rabshakeh, a man from the inside, manipulatively skews Hezekiah's intent and delivers his own people a doomsday message from the outside. How *real life*.

Ginny: I remember a season when I was given advice from the inside that I didn't know how to handle. From the beginning of my music career, I have been offered opportunities to perform at some pretty significant events outside the realm of Christian music. At first, my record label and I were so excited for the unique exposure that we never considered that my involvement would be controversial.

During a radio interview to promote an upcoming show, the DJ asked me, "How do you feel, knowing protesters will be picketing your concert this weekend?" I was stunned and completely caught off guard. I momentarily forgot I was on the air and began asking for details, apologizing profusely for anything I had done to cause the trouble. I learned that several well-known religious leaders around the country had included my name on a list of artists they thought should be boycotted because of my participation in the Nashville stop on the Lilith Fair tour, an enormous all-female music festival tour naturally representing a wide range of musical genres and belief systems. This caused some Christians to assume that I held many beliefs I didn't hold at all. I didn't want to upset anyone, but I also found the idea preposterous that I shouldn't perform for mainstream audiences.

Everyone in my corner of the Christian music world agreed with me. "They're idiots," they said. "Those people just enjoy a good fight. Perhaps they aren't even Christians at all." At the same time, wise, well-meaning friends and family advised me to be careful not to offend the wrong people. They said I should consider taking stances on issues and speak more boldly about my faith so that it would be obvious that I was a Christian. They encouraged me to use words and phrases which would make my Christianity more obvious and to refer to God as "the Lord" instead, because "God" sounded much more vague and universal.

I was torn. I wanted my faith to be apparent, but I didn't want to use often misunderstood phraseology that might distract non-Christians from listening or engaging. I kept thinking, *Have you heard my lyrics?*

I don't think their stance was necessarily wrong. After all, I had chosen to write, record, and market a record to a Christian audience, and without my personal relationship with Jesus I would have nothing to sing about. But neither do I think it was entirely right. I continue to wrestle with the issue of secular versus Christian, and my struggle will forever be colored by the boycott list and the accompanying confusing advice from the inside.

OPEN YOUR EARS, SHUT YOUR MOUTH

Andrew: While my brother was internally reeling from the side effects of postponing a wedding, a decision he cautiously realized was deeply spiritually influenced, he sought out mental and emotional support to affirm his conviction. He needed friends to hear him out as he discerned whether it was God or some emotionally skewing spirit pranking his feelings into believing that his and Kerry's wedding was the wrong idea, or at least at the wrong time.

During these sensitive few weeks leading up to the engagement's end, Chris was a full-time employee at his church. Being surrounded by a staff and congregation of Christians, he was offered unsolicited, spiritually-charged advice by plenty of well-meaning folks. Unfortunately, he also too often found himself an audience of overactive mouths and underactive ears.

Chris's situation was like Ginny's during her musical conundrums. This advice was stemming from folks on the inside, folks who shared similar beliefs with Chris, but their comments lacked the unbiased space and grace he needed to approach the road ahead with confident surrender. And much like Sennacherib's wily message to the Israelites, Chris's friends' hurried advice to do what was best in that moment was shortsighted and shallow. They unknowingly undermined the bigger picture that Chris was painfully trying to discover and trust.

The well-intended advice did not take into account his and Kerry's growing, albeit confusing, love for each other—a persevering love like that which the letter of I Peter encourages oppressed Christians in ancient Asia to exhibit towards each other ("love each other steadily and unselfishly, because love makes up for many faults" [4:8])—and it shortchanged the infinite provisional possibilities that an omniscient and caring Creator might be preparing.

It may sound basic, but perhaps God's greatest redemptive moments rarely result in feeling better today. For those of us who are walking alongside friends trudging through the trenches of doubt and depression, there is wisdom here. Submitting to an eternal and more holistic perspective and encouraging those we love similarly often requires learning when not to speak.

SACRIFICE OF SILENCE: WHEN NOT TO SPEAK AND TO GRIEVE

READ ISAIAH 36:11–22.

[11]Eliakim, Shebna, and Joah appealed to the Rabshakeh.

Hezekiah's Men: Please speak to us, your servants, in a language we understand—Aramaic—not in Judah's common language, so that the people on the wall who are trying to listen in can't understand.

Rabshakeh: [12]*My, my, my!* Do you think that my king sent me here to speak only to your king and to you *when those people stand just as much to lose as you*? Don't you think that these people along the wall should have a chance to hear *our negotiations*? After all, they'll be reduced with you to eating their own feces and drinking their own urine.

[13]So the Rabshakeh stood up and spoke even louder in the Judean language *so all could hear and understand.*

Rabshakeh: Hear the words of Great King *Sennacherib*, king of Assyria, *dominator of the world!*

[14]"Don't listen to Hezekiah's lies. Your king won't be able to save you. [15]Don't let him convince you to trust the Eternal by saying, 'The Eternal will surely save us; God will spare Jerusalem from the king of Assyria.' [16]Don't believe it *for a minute.*"

My king, *Sennacherib*, says, "Make your peace with me. *Don't fight it,* but come on out and join me. Then each of you will be able to *enjoy your home and garden,* eat your own grapes and figs, and drink the water from your own cistern [17]until I come and bring you *back to my place.* Oh, it's like yours, to be sure. It has grain for bread and vineyards for new wine. [18]Be careful or Hezekiah will deceive you with his *empty* claim: 'The Eternal One will *surely* save us.' *Look around.* We've defeated everyone we've fought—*every capital of every country.* And did their gods save them? *No.* [19]Where are the gods of Hamath and Arpad, Sepharvaim, or even *your sibling to the north,* Samaria? [20]All of these are fallen—not a god *in sight* to save them. *Do you really think you're so different?* Why should the Eternal save Jerusalem from me?"

[21]*To their credit*, the people didn't say anything. Hezekiah had commanded them not to answer *the Rabshakeh, and indeed they just sat there silently.* [22]Then *the three men who had gone for Hezekiah*—Hilkiah's son Eliakim, the palace administrator; Shebna, the royal secretary; and

Asaph's son Joah, the recorder—returned to their king. *In great distress, they tore their clothes and told him everything the Rabshakeh said.*

WHEN NOT TO SPEAK

Andrew: In the modern Western world, silence is considered a sign of weakness, of rolling over and taking it. Silence has been a cultural misconception throughout history. The early bird gets the worm; the loudmouth gets heard. But Judah's silence was an exhibition of strength, a declaration of their allegiance and utter dependence on something steadier than their current situation—a trust in someone with an eternal vantage point. It was an act of *faith*.

After an onslaught of activity, including Hezekiah's three Judean messengers being diminished by the Rabshakeh's obstinate and loud declaration of Sennacherib's manipulative threats and the swift conquest of Judah's protective cities, the Judean people answer simply with silence (v. 12–21). Rather than react to the here and now, Judah settles into a broader, eternal perspective.

This posture opposes today's self-help pop culture that demands our rights to immediate satisfaction and instant resolution. Patient response requires faith, and faith is a widely underrated and under-exercised action in our modern belief systems.

During their separation, Chris and Kerry hurt each other as they navigated the tumult of an uncertain future. Their behaviors were not one hundred per- cent loving or conducive to building a future together. Because of this, some counsel advised Chris and Kerry individually to

> **Judah's silence was an exhibition of strength, a declaration of their allegiance and utter dependence on something steadier than their current situation.**

completely sever the relationship even though each expressed clear interest in the long-term possibilities. On the other hand, others encouraged increased engagement when they were sensing the need for or seeking time and space to give the long term a fighting chance. Again, few listened. Many talked.

In receiving and understanding this disparate advice from family, friends, and counselors, my brother, like Judah, exercised caution. In my conversations with Chris, he often did not reply, not out of disagreement or apathy, I discovered, but because he was out of options. His feelings didn't help. Kerry couldn't help. And reciting tenets of the faith or Scripture was cold and calculated. Like the Judeans during their time of tumult, Chris was humbly and desperately seeking authentic clarity in clouds of confusion. And so, he was simply quiet.

TO GRIEVE

Andrew: In verse 22, the three men that Hezekiah sent to receive the Rabshakeh's message—Eliakim, Shebna, and Joah—tore their clothes as they delivered Sennacherib's aggravated declaration to Hezekiah. While I prefer to keep my clothes on in the midst of grief, in ancient Jewish culture tearing one's garments had dual symbolism. The act was a humble expression of desperation and grief when mourning the loss of a loved one. It also illustrated belief in the spiritual realm, the hope that after death we trade our temporal body for an eternal soul.

In today's culture, dramatic expressions of mourning are perceived as inappropriate or uncomfortable for others, as if dealing with physical and emotional deaths—realities our culture works hard to stave off and ignore—is simple and void of complexities. Grief is often overlooked. Perhaps this discomfort of such an elemental and important human experience is a sign of a culture that has lost hope. Perhaps the inability to lean into grief is indicative of people who have little to no assurance of a greater, eternal design. An appropriate season of mourning is a healthy juncture between remembering and moving forward. Sure, we participate in tradition. We ceremonially bury the dead. We memorialize with epitaphs and eulogies. Then we go back to work, attend church, sit down for dinner as if the floor didn't just fall out from under our feet. Some die old and ready. But some die young and very much alive. In each scenario, we who are still mortal are faced with the great mysterious unknown. No matter what our spiritual convictions or doctrinal doubts, death affects us all.

Hezekiah's messengers are shredding their clothes in sadness over the news of the disastrous Assyrian intentions and how this will affect their people's emotional and physical security. They are distraught and they are not afraid to show it. In Isaiah 37:1, even the king tears his clothes, dons sackcloth, and enters the temple to grieve and seek guidance. Just as it is a gesture of sadness and holding out hope for a recent loss, it is also a symbol of surrender for Hezekiah and his men as they live with the Assyrian's obstinate threats and reach out to God for help.

As Chris processed and learned and decided and lived in the depression of not knowing, he figuratively tore his clothes day in and day out. He sought help from a counselor. He grieved on the phone with his brother. And in surrender, he began to place more of his hope in the ultimate outcome—immortality with the Eternal—than in a short-term solution.

When the spiritual realm burrows deep and abides in vulnerable places, it is difficult to explain or even exhibit how intangible truths sustain us during ununderstandable seasons. And as our fight turns to quiet, we begin to trust the mystery of God's character and are inexorably drawn to His presence in the middle of our darkest scenes.

Q&A:
The Process of Grief

Andrew: How has the process of grief played a role in your spiritual life?

Ginny: It isn't grief but my response to grief that impacts my spiritual life. When my mother was battling cancer several years ago, I moved home to help her manage the treatments. Just before she began chemotherapy, her father, who had been in poor health for several years, was admitted to the hospital. I remember flying in after a weekend of concerts, going straight to Grandpa's bedside, and promising him that I would take care of Mom. The next morning, he passed away. Two days later, Mom began her cancer treatment.

Thinking about it now brings tears to my eyes, but at the time I fought hard to keep from feeling any strong emotion. I needed to remain calm, even, and responsible. Grief would only get in the way. Throughout my mom's treatment, I held fast to my false strength.

In hindsight, I understand that the numbness which I forced upon my heart made it impossible for me to receive strength from God or support from anyone else. I wonder what He might have taught me during that season if I had allowed myself to grieve.

QUESTIONS
for Reflection

1. How would you have responded to the Rabshakeh's claim that "your God, the Eternal, sent me" (v. 10)? When have you encountered people who did something wrong while claiming that it was God's will? When have you done this yourself?

2. Put verses 18–20 into your own words. What claims is the Rabshakeh making? What is he saying about God, the Eternal? How would you have reacted if you'd been listening from the top of the city walls?

3. Why do the ambassadors of Judah tear their clothes (v. 22)? Does their grief indicate that they don't trust God, or something else? How have you expressed grief in your own life?

MINE EYES

(Words and Music: Andrew Greer and Emily DeLoach)

He gave us bones
He gave us blood
He gave us heart
To feel everything
I've felt the break
I've stopped the pulse
Prayed it away
Still no relief
Mine eyes look to the hills
Asking You how to feel
Shade my right hand
Say You're near
I did what I did
With thoughtful care
Thought with my heart
Got me nowhere
She followed my lead
Promised her hand
Even my doubts
Won't let me leave

© 2012 Mr. Andy's Music / ASCAP

CHAPTER 6

WHAT YOU BELIEVE

> "You don't have to
> scream and shout to
> let your voice be heard
> / You've gotta live
> what you believe . . ."
>
> —Ginny Owens and Monroe
> Jones, "What You Believe"

> "So long as we are
> occupied with any
> other object than God
> Himself, there will
> be neither rest for
> the heart nor peace
> for the mind."
>
> —A. W. Pink,
> *The Sovereignty of God*

Ginny: As a child, one of my favorite fictional characters was Cornelia VanTwerp. She lived in a haunted house, owned a mischievous pet pig, wore very high heels and always found herself in the midst of some delightfully terrifying adventure. Ever hear of her? Probably not, since she was the creation of my grandfather's vivid imagination. Miss VanTwerp primarily existed during my elementary school years when my grandparents lived in a beautiful historic manse in a lovely, old-established section of Montgomery, Alabama, just a few tree-lined blocks from the church with the big columns where Grandpa was pastor.

When my mom, brother, and I would visit on vacation, we and any other grandkids present would spend the evening meal begging for Cornelia stories. After plenty of pleading, Grandpa would finally promise that if we would pipe down and clean our plates, he would grant our wish. After dinner, he would turn off the lights and all of us cousins would settle in on the large carpeted staircase, entranced as Grandpa delivered one frightening Cornelia tale after another. Being a storyteller myself, how he came up with those plots and characters on the spot is beyond me, but he did. And I loved every minute of it.

My Grandpa and I were big buddies and kindred spirits. Perhaps it was because I was the oldest of fourteen grandchildren and had several years to get to know him on my own before anyone else came along to vie for his attention. Or perhaps it was because he and I were the resident introverts, inevitably retreating to the same corner after several hours of holiday family fun.

Besides Cornelia tales, my fondest childhood memories of Grandpa involved music. As I plunked out hymns on our piano, he would pull up a chair beside me and audaciously sing along. Duets were more challenging than it sounds, since I could only play by ear in a few keys, and he had a lower voice. But he poured his heart and soul into every word. I can still hear his rich baritone voice straining for the high notes, courageously declaring the song of the saints who had gone before, words that were nearer to his heart than almost any others.

I can also hear his voice from behind the pulpit: booming, forceful, persuasive, issuing a stern edict to his congregants. His sermons were intense. He was never afraid to confront listeners with the truth that he found in his Bible, even when what he discovered was unpopular and uncomfortable. He insisted on living by his convictions, but his countenance was most often gentle, thoughtful, and sensitive. When there was church drama, he insisted on prayer and communication to resolve the conflict, avoiding negative measures as often as possible.

Sometimes sticking to his guns resulted in less than leisurely living for him and his family. At one of his pastorates, he refused a salary increase, saying, "Not until we're giving away as much as we're taking in."

A self-proclaimed "unlikely candidate for ministry," Grandpa attended church sporadically while growing up in Iowa but had no personal faith. The ingenious methods he came up with for making money—getting hired by the circus when he was eleven, managing a paper route at twelve, and playing his cornet in dance bands at local bars as a college student—seemed to forecast a career in business or perhaps music, but not ministry.

But during his freshman year of college, he found himself searching for deeper meaning in life. A former band director shared with him about salvation through Jesus, and from that moment on he was, in his words, "On fire for the Lord." He talked about his fresh faith with anyone who would listen. He papered his entire college campus with Christian literature. And he placed a sign in the back window of his old Chevrolet declaring, "Prepare to meet thy God!"

Grandpa took this newfound fervor for the Lord into the Army Air Corps, where his World War II duties involved flying in the back of bombers attached by a single strap to the airplane floor. After fulfilling his military service, Grandpa traded his small town roots for the big city of Los Angeles, where he eventually married my grandmother. Grandpa finished pursuing his business degree

"The Lord had something other than a good job, nice house, and typical life for us."

and began working for Prudential, all the while continuing his passionate pursuit of God.

Before long, he and Grandma became very involved at church, teaching Sunday School, working with the youth, hosting Bible studies and prayer groups in their home, and volunteering in Fellowship of the Burning Hearts, a college evangelism group and Campus Crusade precursor. Grandma says she never planned on being a pastor's wife, but "more and more, we were feeling that the Lord had something other than a good job, nice house, and typical life for us." So against everyone else's better judgment, Grandpa gave up his insurance job and went back to school.

Upon graduating with honors from Fuller Seminary, my grandpa received his first church call to a congregation of forty in a tiny rural Mississippi town. As they researched Woodville, all my grandparents could find were old reports indicating no running water and no inside plumbing. Unafraid of a little outside flush, Grandpa and Grandma packed up their family and their belongings and left Los Angeles County to begin their adventures in ministry.

My sense has always been that my grandparents didn't look to the left or the right much, but instead focused on what God placed before them to do. Grandpa was well loved and humble, shepherding each of his congregants graciously and faithfully. Study and prayer were key elements of his daily life. And he and my grandmother raised five children on a modest salary and daily devotions. Fanfare did not characterize their ministry—their relationship with God did, and their courage to tell others about Him.

COMMUNION WITH GOD: HONOR AND OBEDIENCE AND FAITHFULNESS

READ 1 KINGS 17:1–10.

Elijah the Tishbite, one of the Gilead settlers, spoke to Ahab.

Elijah: As the Eternal lives—the True God *who gives life* to the Israelites, the God whom I serve—no rain or dew will touch the earth unless I give word.

²The Eternal One gave him this message:

Eternal One: ³*I want you to* travel away from this place and go east. Keep yourself hidden near the Cherith stream, east of the Jordan. ⁴You will have water from the stream *during this drought,* and I will tell the birds to take care of you *while you are hiding* there.

⁵Elijah did just as the Eternal had instructed him to do. He lived near the Cherith stream, east of the Jordan. ⁶The ravens *did take care of him while he was there, just as the Lord said,* bringing him a meal of bread and meat at sunrise and *another meal of* bread and meat at sunset. He *satisfied his thirst by* drinking from the stream. ⁷Soon the stream became dry because of the drought.

⁸The Eternal One gave him this message:

Eternal One: ⁹Get up, and travel to Zarephath. It is in the possession of Sidon, *which is outside Israel.* Remain there, *and do not leave for any reason.* There is a widow in Zarephath whom I have told to take care of you.

¹⁰Elijah got up and *immediately* traveled to Zarephath. He arrived at the city gate, and at that moment, a widow was picking up sticks nearby.

HONOR

Ginny: Elijah's courage to deliver confrontational messages to Israel's wayward people and powerful rulers places him near the top of my list of biblical heroes. Who walks up to a king and declares a drought in his kingdom? The protagonist in a fairy tale might do this, or an insane person perhaps—or a man whose courage comes from somewhere outside himself.

When Elijah shows up on the scene, God's people are mired in flagrant behavior that directly defies the Eternal and their spiritual welfare. The Israelites keep denying God. And Ahab, Israel's seventh king since the nation split into the Northern Kingdom (Israel) and the Southern Kingdom (Judah), is one in a long line of unscrupulous monarchs.

The writer of 1 Kings refers to Ahab several times as doing "more evil in the eyes of the LORD than any of those before him" (16:30 NIV). For starters, he marries Jezebel, a cruel, vengeful princess from the pagan nation of Sidon, who becomes famous for killing off the Eternal's prophets. Persuaded by his wife's worship preferences, the king and queen pay homage to Baal, a rain god popular in Jezebel's homeland, and Asherah, a goddess of fertility (1 Kings 16:30–33; 18:13). The majority of Ahab's subjects follow suit. Because he has no regard for the Eternal, Ahab allows Hiel, a man from Bethel, to rebuild the city of Jericho, bury his eldest son under its foundation to ensure favor from the gods, and bury his youngest son under the gates to ward off evil. This superstitious behavior and direct disobedience to the Eternal fulfills an oath that Joshua made several centuries earlier that the man who rebuilt Jericho, the city God delivered to the Israelites through Joshua's obedient seven-day march, would be cursed by God and lose his sons in the rebuilding (16:34; Joshua 6:26).

It seems that Elijah's career is characterized as much by the way he reveres, defers to, and worships the Lord as it is by the miracles he is so famous for.

Because of this successive line of destructive kings, God has a very specific mission for Elijah: to speak His truth to King Ahab and Israel in an attempt to draw the Israelites back to Him. So in our introduction to Elijah, he is embarking on this restoration quest, delivering the bold message of a drought until further notice to Ahab on behalf of the Eternal (1 Kings 17:1).

I'm as fascinated by what the Bible does not tell us as by what it does. We are given no account of Elijah's first interactions with the Lord, no explanations of how the Eternal revealed Himself to Elijah, and no "You want me to do what?" exclamations from Elijah. Instead, our first encounter with the daring prophet finds him declaring to a non-believing king his allegiance to the Eternal. One translation of Elijah's name means "Yahweh is my God." As a prophet, Elijah will surrender his entire life and message to this Yahweh. He will serve this God. In his announcement to Ahab, Elijah pronounces the Eternal as "the God . . . before whom I stand" (NKJV). In the Living Bible, he declares the Lord as the "God whom I worship and serve" (17:1). His reverence for God is apparent. His allegiance to the Eternal is definitive.

My Grandpa's no-nonsense, truth-telling approach reminds me of Elijah. The fearless prophet is faithful to the Eternal and fiercely courageous on His behalf. Elijah's prophetic career is full of miracles. His boldness was undoubtedly divinely inspired, but he, too, was human with his own thoughts, feelings, and free will. And when I wonder how Elijah found the superhuman courage to confront a king, I study the way he honors God.

"Honor" is an old word, and perhaps an old concept, that doesn't hold much weight in today's society. I can't even find an equivalent word in modern vocabulary. Google dictionary says that to "honor" is to "regard with great respect," and its synonyms include "defer to," "worship," and to "revere."[1] It seems that Elijah's career is characterized as much by the way he reveres, defers to, and worships the Lord as it is by the miracles he is so famous for conducting. For him, God takes precedence over all else: where he will reside, what he will eat, and what the next part of his mission will look like. Elijah's reverence for the Lord allows him to let worries and questions take a back seat to the Eternal's divine plans.

When I consider Elijah's total surrender to God's big picture plans, I am left contemplating: *What does it look like to honor the Lord in my everyday life? How do I give His Word and His truth precedence in my journey? How do I create space for Him to speak and lead?* These things are not because I feel I have to but because I have come to know Him as the true God. And if He is truly God, doesn't He deserve ultimate honor?

OBEDIENCE AND FAITHFULNESS

Ginny: As we observe the interplay between Elijah and the Eternal, scene after scene, God directs Elijah, and Elijah obeys. The relationship between God and Elijah is portrayed so simply and beautifully. I wish my journey of faith looked like this. The Eternal leads; Elijah follows.

After delivering a message of drought to a king who worships a rain god, God provides Elijah a hiding place where he most likely remained for at least a year. If I had been Elijah, concealed in secret for over a year, I would have found all kinds of things to worry about. Would I be discovered? How long would I have to stay? What happens when the stream dries up? I would have come up with a Plan B—but not Elijah. He defies logic and stays put, doing "just as the Eternal had instructed him to do" (v. 5). The Divine Orchestrator then sends Elijah to a land outside of Israel where he's never been, to live with a widow he doesn't know, and instead of asking for more details, he simply goes. (Ironically, the widow God sends Elijah to seek refuge with lives in Sidon, Jezebel's old homeland, and she may have been the only God-fearing person there. Once again we see how Elijah's obedience against the odds proves God's faithfulness even in a land of dirty kings and false gods.)

Elijah's obedience speaks loudly to me. "Obey" is not my favorite word. As a creative, the connotation for me is restrictive, like a bird in a cage. The sinner in me doesn't like the idea of obedience much either. When it comes to my relationship with God, I can often behave like the person who looks in the mirror, only to forget what she looks like as soon as she walks away (James 1:23–24). I love the good news of saving grace, but I don't enjoy the practical steps of obedience that grace requires. I want it to be more romantic, more about the intellectual discoveries that come from study or conversation with others. Yet it seems that these cerebral insights have no impact on my relationship with the Eternal if I don't also choose to surrender to Him by heeding His inspired instructions in Scripture or asking for His divine guidance. As I see how Elijah's trusting responses keep him safe, cared for, and on the quest God has created for him, I am inspired to also respond with obedience.

In my grandparents' ministry, obedience seemed to be an ever-present theme. Though their friends and family questioned and did not support their decision to attend seminary, they went anyway, believing that if seminary had been impressed on their hearts by God, He would provide. When Grandpa's first preaching position was at a tiny southern church two thousand miles away from home, they went, trusting that God would be faithful in

> I love the good news of saving grace, but I don't enjoy the practical steps of obedience that grace requires.

their new season. Being from the more integrated Los Angeles societies, the intense racial prejudices of a southern black-versus-white culture—even being derogatorily referred to by community folks as "the Yankees"—was a culture shock. But they pressed in to God, staying the course until they felt him leading elsewhere. When the Lord opened and closed doors and sent them on to other pastorates, they packed up their growing family, left their friends behind, and trusted God. Grandpa's denomination went through a dramatic split, and he found himself in the midst of many impassioned opinions—but he prayed, waited, and relied on the Lord's faithfulness to guide him through the strained change.

I wonder if Elijah trusted God upon his first encounter with Him, or if his trust in God developed as he obeyed. In my experience with God, trust in Him grows as I take steps of obedience. As my grandparents obeyed again and again, their trust in the Eternal deepened, because again and again they experienced God's faithfulness.

Probing this passage even deeper, the interaction between Elijah and the Eternal is not one-sided. Both God and Elijah are faithful in their pursuit of each other. In fact, God is pursuing His people by pursuing Elijah. As He prepares Elijah for his upcoming encounters with fickle Israel and the people's propensity to pursue false gods, He reveals to Elijah what the true God's faithfulness looks like: He cares for him at every turn; He gives him an undiscovered hiding place next to a stream for drinking water; nature's Creator sends birds to deliver Elijah's food each day; and when the stream dries up and Ahab and his kingdom search for Elijah (18:10), the Lord has already instructed him to move. Elijah has experienced how steps of obedience open up the floodgate of God's faithfulness, and can now share his experiences—his testimony—with the obstinate Israelites personally.

PROVING THE TRUE GOD: ASK THE HARD QUESTIONS AND SURRENDER

READ 1 KINGS 18:1–2, 17–29.

Many days passed, and the word of the Eternal visited Elijah during the third year *of the drought.*

Eternal One: Go now, and reveal yourself to Ahab. *When you do,* I will bring rain on the earth.

²Elijah then went to reveal himself to Ahab. . . .

Ahab *(seeing Elijah)*: ¹⁷There you are. *I thought I perceived* a trouble-maker in Israel.

Elijah: ¹⁸*Hypocrite!* I have caused no mischief in Israel. It is you and your family who are guilty *of the very thing you accuse me of.* You have turned your back on the laws of the Eternal *and abandoned your devotion to Him. Instead* you have given yourselves to the Baals, *the masters of pagan nations.* ¹⁹Now I want you to gather the entire community of Israel and send them to Mount Carmel to meet with me. *I have a message for them.* Be sure to gather the 450 prophets of Baal and the 400 prophets of *the goddess* Asherah—the ones who fill their mouths *and stomachs* with food from Jezebel's table.

²⁰Ahab *did as Elijah asked,* sent word throughout the entire community of Israel, and gathered all the prophets atop Mount Carmel.

Elijah *(approaching the people)*: ²¹How much longer will you sit on the fence, refusing to make a decision *between the Lord and Baal*? If *you believe* the Eternal One is the True God, then devote yourselves entirely to Him. If *you believe* Baal is your master, then devote yourselves entirely to him.

All the people *who were gathered together atop Mount Carmel* were completely silent. *They didn't know what to say to this.*

Elijah: ²²I am the last remaining prophet of the Eternal. Baal has 450 prophets. *Let us do a test to reveal the true quality of our deities.* ²³Bring us two young bulls, *the common sacrifice to your master whom you depict as a bull.* The prophets of Baal may choose *first* which bull they want. They will *kill it,* chop it up, and *prepare it for a fire* by placing it above wood; but they will not light it. I will do the same with the other bull and prepare it *for fire* and place it above wood, but I will not light it. ²⁴Then you call upon your god, *Baal,* and I will call upon the Eternal. The God who answers with fire is the one True God.

Everyone *liked this idea and* said, "This sounds like a worthy plan."

Elijah *(to the prophets of Baal)***:** ²⁵You have the pick of the bulls. Take the one you want, and prepare it first because there are many of you. Call upon your god, but do not set fire to the wood.

²⁶The prophets of Baal picked out their bull and prepared it. They called upon Baal from dawn till noon, crying out, "Baal, answer us *with fire!*" But there was no voice, no reply. *Nothing happened.* All they did was dance around the altar they had built *and cry out to an elusive god.*
²⁷At about midday, Elijah began provoking them.

Elijah: You have to shout louder than that! The one to whom you cry out certainly must be a god! Perhaps he is daydreaming or napping or away from his *heavenly* throne. Perhaps he is in a deep sleep, and you must wake him up. *Shout louder!*

²⁸So all the prophets of Baal began to shout at the top of their lungs *pleading with all their might.* They cut themselves with knives and swords *and spears* until they were covered in their own blood. ²⁹Midday passed by, and the prophets of Baal kept on with their antics until it was time for the evening sacrifice. But *still,* there was no voice, no reply. No god heard them.

ASK THE HARD QUESTIONS

Ginny: The other day while getting my nails done, I had the most fascinating conversation with Christine, the Vietnamese nail technician. She began our chat by sharing that this day was the start of the Vietnamese New Year. She described to me how she and her family celebrated the holiday. Many prayers were offered to Buddha for good luck, health, and prosperity, and special food was placed in front of a statue of the ancient sage residing in the kitchen. Christine collected Buddhas and other gods to place around her house for good fortune, and she had just found a smiling elephant that she felt good about adding to her living room. Christine also loved feng shui, a "system of harmonizing the human existence with the surrounding environment,"[2] or creating spaces that radiate positive energy and invite good vibes. "Did you know there are feng shuis for everything?" she asked enthusiastically. "Even for health and career!"

She later told me that she attends church because, as she said, church is an especially good training ground for children since the church teaches the Bible. I was thoroughly fascinated. I have never had such an in-depth conversation with a religious pluralist.

Several years ago, I became acquainted with the concept of "religious pluralism." Maybe I was late to the game, but when I first read the term in a Bible study, I had to look it up. Even after reading its definition, grasping its meaning and its relevance to our culture required some thought.

The Oxford Dictionary defines pluralism as "a theory or system that recognizes more than one ultimate principle."[3] Paramount in a religiously pluralistic society is respecting the otherness of others and accepting the given uniqueness endowed to each one of us. Though I never heard my grandfather preach about pluralism, the term was becoming a recurring theme in the sermons and writings I came across as an adult. I grew up under the impression that I lived in a predominantly Christian nation, so viewing our nation as a religiously pluralistic society was a bit of a paradigm-shift for me.

Like Israel, we live in a society where endless numbers of religions exist. We choose one, none, or a combination of several to guide us, depending on personal convictions. Pluralism claims that we can choose our own path regardless of others, and the ultimate guiding principles in a pluralistic society are tolerance and acceptance of everyone. So in order for us to tolerate or accept so many preferences, we often utilize relativism, the notion that all religions are good and lead to the same end—a circular thought that eventually nullifies the validity of every religion. In *Pluralism as a Religious Philosophy*, Charles Garland highlights the weary loopholes of relativism by contending, "Relativism . . . fights to make sure no one believes in any absolutes while they must use their own absolute to establish this idea."[4]

When my convictions oppose someone else's convictions, I often feel my hands are tied. Instead of having a healthy discourse on our differences, more times than I care to admit, my irresoluteness eventually becomes indifference.

I struggle with what tolerance and acceptance should look like. On one hand, I resent obnoxious, loud, ungracious Christians who wear their spirituality as a badge to lambaste those who do not share their views. At the same time, I feel ill equipped to debate the finer points of my Christian discipleship with those of different religions. To avoid offending someone who is expressing beliefs different from mine,

> If I do believe that the Eternal is the true God, would I not want to find ways of initiating dialogue with others about Him?

I often nod, smile, politely hear them out, and gently change the subject before things get too uncomfortable, hoping that my kindness will reflect God's love. Sounds a bit absurd, doesn't it? Fortunately, Elijah's story offers me insight.

In verse 18, we find Elijah again confronting Ahab with his sin. But this time, he wants to engage the entire Northern Kingdom in understanding the error of its ways. He insists that Ahab convene Baal's and Asherah's prophets to meet with him in a public battle of the gods. Although I wouldn't propose a Madison Square Garden-sized conference gathering our nation together for a competition of religions, this passage speaks to me about initiating conversation with those who don't believe as I do. If I do believe that the Eternal is the true God, would I not want to find ways of initiating dialogue with others about Him? If I believe that trusting Him is the only right way, would it not be helpful for me to discourse with those who believe otherwise?

When the people show up for this epic convention, Elijah boldly calls them out for refusing to choose whom they will serve (v. 21). Some translations of this verse express his pleading: "How long will you sit on the fence?" "How long will you hobble at the crossroads?"[5] "How long will you waver between two opinions?"(NIV). In the words of American Christian apologist Timothy Keller, Elijah was warning the Israelites that to "presume the delusion of neutrality . . . is the worst possible place to stand."[6]

Just as in our current culture, when every god is acceptable there is no need to worship one in particular. Unlike Elijah's explicit worship of the Eternal, many of the Israelites possessed no loyalty to either god. They sometimes worshipped Baal; they sometimes sacrificed to the Lord. It was relative, depending on what seemed right to them. So Elijah calls them out on their inability to commit to serve only one God, and silence falls.

To test which "god" is real—the God with one prophet or the god with 450—Elijah proposes a test. As a gesture of good faith, he gives the prophets of Baal the advantage. The sacrifice will be a bull, a common sacrifice to Baal, and they get to handpick the bull. Whichever god consumes the sacrifice with fire is the true God. The people agree—perhaps because of their lack of allegiance to any god or because of their fickle nature—and the contest ensues (vv. 22–24).

Even though my grandfather didn't have to deal with physical false gods, he was faced with the challenge of serving people whose hearts tended to chase other gods, including having to deal with his own heart at times. As I read about Elijah's interaction with the Israelites here, I realize how quickly and easily my heart becomes like theirs. More than I care to admit, I worship at the altar of my busyness, my insecurities, and my desires. And like Elijah challenging the Israelites, I must put these idols to the test so I can be reminded again how they compare to the one true God.

SURRENDER?

Ginny: Ever since I can remember, my grandparents have left religious tracts with their tips at restaurants. I have witnessed them walk many people through the four points of the plan of salvation. And while I respect these methods of communicating their Christian beliefs, I often find that sharing my faith is a prayerful, intentional process that can require years. My deepest desire for my friends and acquaintances who don't yet know Christ is for them to experience His life-changing peace and freedom. Yet I often find that the best way to convey His heart to those in my space and further discover it myself is to live transparently with them, pray for them, and listen and wait as the false gods prove themselves ineffective in each of our lives. They always do.

As Elijah stands by, idols drive the prophets crazy. Elijah begins provoking the prophets until they are frantic, perhaps because he has a flair for the dramatic, or perhaps because he wants the people to see the contest's futility. As he watches and waits, the prophets of Baal begin to unravel, showcasing for the Israelites the problem with serving a master other than the Eternal. Prayers become hysterical screams. There is no answer. Animal sacrifice is followed by shedding of the prophets' own blood. Still there is no response. The prophets' suppositions grow into chaotic stress. But yet, no answer, no fire, no god (vv. 27–29).

There is something here that I cannot miss: when I give all of my heart, time, and attention to anything or anyone other than God, I unravel in the same misinformed manner, beginning with restlessness and anxiety and ending in chaos. Because I grant something or some-one authority who does not have ultimate power, I come undone. My false gods don't love me; they enslave me, and they answer my prayers with silence.

Andrew: There is a relentless resistance to surrender among modern people. Perhaps that statement is a bit nearsighted, considering that human nature—and I am most human—throughout the course of history has shifted between self-re-liance or self-fulfillment and yielding to a higher power. I am satisfied with my effectiveness when

> My false gods don't love me; they enslave me, and they answer my prayers with silence.

the power of control feels within my grip, when the ship responds to the helm, when what I worship produces what I want to achieve. But when push comes to shove or my ship is taking on water, I understand firsthand my need for help. And I am acutely aware that the help I need is not within my capabilities or the empty substances of financial gain, power, marriage—whatever it is we worship other than God.

I understand why surrender is so unpopular. It's countercultural, maybe even counterintuitive based on what our environment teaches us. In terms of everyday living, surrender means giving up, resigning, acquiescing to the demands or triumphs of someone we don't agree with and probably don't like. Even in the church, among evangelicals, postmodernists, or any other variation of Christian views prevalent today, we encourage a rhetoric of self-betterment and achievement—name it and claim it. You know the drill. Even humanitarianism without a bigger-picture purpose can be a pat on the back for me and a detriment to the person being served.

But when we pause, lay down our drive to get it done, and seek ultimate satisfaction from a Creator with eternal perspective, our heart and mind begin to respond from the core of our soul, where God speaks. And not only do we understand ourselves and direction better, but we become more attuned to the needs of others and love God better through the process of both.

WORSHIPING THE TRUE GOD: LIVE VULNERABLY AND PRAY BOLDLY

READ 1 KINGS 18:30–39.

Elijah *(to the people)*: [30]Gather around me.

So all the people gathered around him, and he fixed the Eternal's altar that had been torn down. [31]Elijah gathered 12 stones, one for each of Jacob's tribes. Jacob was the one who *wrestled with God and whom* the word of the Eternal One visited, saying, "Your name will be Israel."

[32]Elijah took the *12* stones and constructed an altar in honor of the Eternal One and carved a ditch out around it large enough to hold 13 quarts of seed. [33]He set up the wood, chopped up the bull, and placed it on top of the wood.

Elijah *(to the people)*: Go get four big jars, and fill them all up with water. Then pour the water out over the burnt offering and the wood. [34]*Now, do the same thing again.*

And so they did it a second time.

Elijah: *All right,* now do the same thing a third time.

And so they did it a third time. [35]The water covered the altar and even filled up the ditch. [36]When it was time for offering the evening sacrifice, Elijah called out *to the Eternal.*

Elijah *(praying)*: Eternal One—God of Abraham, Isaac, and Israel— reveal Yourself on this day as Israel's God. Make it known that I serve You and have done all this because You commanded it *of me.* [37]Answer me, Eternal One. Reveal Yourself so that everyone here will know that You, Eternal One, are the True God—*the only God. Do it so that everyone knows* You are turning the gaze of their hearts back *to You* again.

[38]Right then the Eternal One's fire landed *upon the altar.* The flames consumed the burnt offering, the wood, the stones, and the ground. The flames even drank up all the water in the ditch. [39]When everyone witnessed this *extraordinary power,* they all put their faces to the ground *in fear and awe and wonder.*

People: The Eternal One is the True God! The Eternal One is the True God!

LIVE VULNERABLY

Ginny: Laying the groundwork was always key in my grandparents' ministry. Aside from their private lives of prayer and study, they poured themselves into their congregations by doing life with them, struggling through hard times and celebrating good news. They also created opportunities for them to grow by serving. Grandpa engaged nearly all of his churches in mission work. Grandma began church-wide and community-wide women's Bible study groups. Most of these endeavors continued long after my grandparents were gone.

Elijah is intentional, setting the scene thoughtfully. He gathers everyone so they won't miss a moment. He repairs the Eternal's altar, which has nearly fallen apart for lack of use. He gathers twelve stones, representing the twelve tribes of Israel, as a symbolic reminder to the Israelites of who they are and whose they are. With these stones and wood, he completes the construction of the altar and centers the sacrifice. As a final handicap, he asks the Israelites to pour twelve jars of water over the altar, perhaps to poignantly represent all the false-god energy that the tribes had exerted to separate themselves from the Eternal (vv. 30–33).

I find Elijah's behavior an encouragement to be transparent on my journey with the Eternal. God's power may be seen and understood more clearly by those around me when my submission to Him is obvious. Telling others about the Lord is one thing, but allowing them to see my vulnerabilities and struggles as I pursue Him could enable them to witness His faithfulness firsthand.

Andrew: Ginny hits on an emotional adjective that has thankfully become more commonplace in the fellowship of Christ-followers in the twenty-first century: "vulnerable." My closest friends who struggle with the influence of the Old Testament and how it seems to portray a wide range of seemingly conflicting characteristics for God were often discouraged in their vulnerable searches for God as young pupils in Sunday schools across America. Raising a reasonable question that might illuminate doubt among their young peers, or even in the teacher, could result in a "because the Bible says so" type of answer, causing a shutdown among a generation of youth vulnerably inquiring about God in order to better identify and relate to Him.

Compounded by home lives that seemed to echo their church's legalism rather than foster environments for graceful questioning, reasoning, and doubting, "vulnerable" was a foreign concept for my friends, and perhaps for you, at least in spiritual matters. As a result, the God who ultimately related to us humans through Jesus, "grief's patient friend" (Isa. 53:3), was unconsciously cut out of our lives.

This was not my experience. But then again, my dad is a therapist, and we grew up "on the couch," encouraged to share our feelings whenever possible. Well, we were still normal, but we felt the freedom to seek because my parents were persuaded by a God who walks with each of us on the road to discovery.

May we always encourage transparency and vulnerability in the fellowship of seekers in the worldwide church, so the church can become a house of confession through conversation and a meeting place between God and us.

PRAY BOLDLY

Ginny: After serving five churches, raising five children, and living long enough to enjoy fourteen grandkids and seven great-grandkids, my grandmother still insists that prayer is the key to her journey. She remembers a time before seminary when the prayer group that met at their home would turn off the lights, kneel in front of their chairs, and ask the Lord to work. "As we cried out to God, things happened," she said. "Some of the group became missionaries to Korea and to Africa. Marriages were reconciled. And several of us went into the ministry."

There is incredible, unknowable power in prayer for those who engage in it and those who observe the effects from it. Elijah begins his prayer by declaring who God is. Just as when we first met him, Elijah acknowledges that he comes in the name of someone greater. The ensuing display of magnificent power will not be about him. He then asks the Almighty to answer his prayer by revealing Himself to His people (vv. 36–37).

The fire came down and consumed everything: the bull, the wood, the stones, the ground, even the water (v. 38). The Israelites worshiped, aware that a true God will always possess ultimate power. Their hearts were once again convinced of His authenticity, and for a brief time they revered Him as Elijah had all along, and God ended the nation's drought.

As I share in the lives of others and discover more about my own life, I am convinced that our hearts long to worship. We intuitively seek to serve someone greater than ourselves. Elijah's story encourages me to consider how I might engage with God to honor, obey, and walk openly with Him in a manner that invites others to witness Him as well.

As we observe the Eternal's faithfulness to Elijah, we also are reminded that false gods are incapable of speaking to us, caring for us, or moving in miraculous ways that change our lives and the lives of those around us. In light of this, I want to continually be aware of and discern false gods as I seek the one true God.

ELIJAH'S LARGER-THAN-LIFE LIFE

Ginny: We usually talk of miracles as New Testament occurrences, but God uses them many times in the Old Testament to remind His people that He is the true God and to woo their hearts to Him. Elijah performs many of these miracles. Discover more astounding ways that God provides for this charismatic prophet in these scriptures:

Read 1 Kings 17:9–24. Not only does the Lord provide a safe place for Elijah to hide and an unexpected supply of food through the willingness of a God-fearing woman, He uses Elijah to do something even more miraculous in her life.

Read 1 Kings 18:42–46. The Lord fulfills His promise to Elijah and blesses His people with rain.

Read 2 Kings 1:1–17: After the people have forgotten the god contest and have returned to their idol worship, the Lord shows them again who the true God is.

Read 2 Kings 2:1–15: When I go to heaven, this is how I want to go!

Q&A:
Miracles or Myth

Andrew: Miracles are a well-debated topic in scriptural study. Do you believe in miracles? And how have they occurred in your life?

Ginny: I am a walking target for major miracle seekers. I have been stopped in parking lots, accosted in restaurants, and cornered after concerts by people who want to pray for the miraculous restoration of my eyesight. I wish I could share with them some perspective: the long list of miracles God has worked in my life, and perhaps in the lives of others, because of my blindness.

QUESTIONS for Reflection

1. What things did God do to provide for Elijah's needs in this passage?

2. When have you seen miraculous provision in your own life? When has God allowed you to experience hardship for a time before showing you the next step?

3. In this dramatic "showdown" between Elijah and the prophets of Baal, why did the spectators remain silent? If you had been there, what would you have been thinking?

4. When have you remained silent rather than speaking out for righteousness? What motivated you? What would you do differently if it happened again?

5. If you had been present, how would you have reacted when fire suddenly poured down from heaven and consumed Elijah's sacrifice and altar? Would you have spoken or remained silent?

WHAT YOU BELIEVE

(Words and Music: Ginny Owens / Monroe Jones)

Everybody stands for somethin'
Even when they say they won't
And everyone who aims for nothin'
Will hit it even when they don't
Oh can't you see, my friends, That life is more
    than this
You've gotta live, live
What you believe, what you believe
And walk, walk in truth
Oh love, love
With all your heart, with all your heart
The world is watching you
So live what you believe
Have you been sitting on the sidelines
Just waiting for the world to change
Hoping that you can make a difference
But finding that you are afraid
Well you don't have to scream and shout
To let your voice be heard
So let your light shine, the way light shines on you
'Cause you might be the only light they ever see
And in your darkest night, hold to what you know
    is true
You've gotta live, gotta live what you believe

CHAPTER 7

HYMN FOR LEAVING

> "Leave behind /
> Everything we've
> known / Each goodbye
> / Aches within
> our souls . . ."
>
> —Andrew Greer and Ben
> Rosenbush, "Hymn for Leaving"

> "Man, when he does not
> grieve, hardly exists."
>
> —Antonio Porchia, *Voces*[1]

> "Give sorrow words;
> the grief that does
> not speak whispers
> the o'er-fraught heart
> and bids it break."
>
> —William Shakespeare[2]

Andrew: In the twenty-first century Western world, we are pressed for time. We pride ourselves on busyness. And when it comes to mourning our losses, we run. Sure, we go to the funeral. We eulogize. We create a touching Facebook post. But we pack our calendar even tighter, smile a little wider, and with bleary eyes push our feelings down even deeper.

This passive reaction to heartbreak is fascinating considering that people of all different cultures throughout much of humanity's timeline have expressed a period of focused grieving to signify the void left by death—whether physical or emotional.

Throughout singer-songwriter Amy Grant's public career resides a distinct awareness of pain, in her own life and in the lives of others. I have heard it in her vulnerable songwriting and traced it in brief conversations backstage. This thread of hopeful heartache has intimately related her to a large and loyal audience of real folks for decades, proof that no matter what our surface demeanor says, our hearts are connected by the common denominator of knowing hurt, sadness, and grief.

In her patchwork memoir *Mosaic*, Amy recounts an unlikely meeting that she and her husband, Vince Gill, had with a Nashville woman on her eighty-ninth birthday. The older woman, a longtime fan of Vince's music, told the couple about the close bond she had built with her mother as a child and the immobilizing depression that kept her in bed for over two years following her mom's death years later. When Amy responded, surprised at the length of her mourning, the wise woman simply said, "You know, you cannot rush grief."[3]

Last winter, Cecil Girard, my mother's dad, died just shy of ninety years old and at the end of a full life. Granddad had been missing my grandmother, his bride of nearly sixty years, since she had made her passage to the other side over ten years ago. His body and mind were beginning to deteriorate, which as a former geologist and man who was always on top of the details must have felt like a living death sentence. As a result, he had been preparing his heart and mind for death for years and even more so in his final months.

Two weeks before he died, Mom visited him at his assisted living apartment in East Texas. When she walked in, Mom found Granddad fully dressed, sitting on top of his made-up bed, crying. My mother has always been a good friend to her parents, so she sat down beside him and held his hand. He was confused, a feeling he came to know well but never accustomed to. He asked my mom, "Why am I crying?" Holding his hand, my sweet mother replied, "I don't know. You must be sad."

As if he was her child, Granddad asked my mother's permission: "Do you think it would be okay if I asked Jesus to take me to heaven tonight?" Two weeks later, Granddad went to sleep never to wake up on this side of life again.

After the news reached my mom's fellow teachers, congregants, and friends, she received plenty of condolences—gracious gestures of kindness, good-hearted sentiments that sounded something like this: "I'm glad he went peacefully" or "What a full life he lived." You've heard the Band-Aid phrases, the attempt to make sense of something so unknowable. When at a loss for words but feeling the need to say something, I, too, have uttered these blasé statements. It's as if even in our lack of knowing what to say we want the grieving to know that we identify with how bad it hurts.

Expressions like these remind us that we are loved by our community and by God. But in our moments of loss, grief is the soothing balm. As the elderly woman mourning her mother's loss for years suggested, the time it takes is the time it takes.

For my mom, she still had to put her father in the ground. During my brother's failed engagement, he was still aching over the mysterious separation between him and his beloved. In Trey and Stephanie's shock with cancer, they were still wondering, thinking, and planning what it might look like to have a household of young girls with no mother. And in the backcountry of Wyoming, my heart was still waiting for some sign that God was real. That He was present. That He cared. So I grieved.

Our hearts are connected by the common denominator of knowing hurt, sadness, and grief.

TO EVERY SEASON: GRIEVE AND ASK

READ ISAIAH 37:1–7.

When King Hezekiah heard the report, *he, too,* was *terribly distressed.* He tore his clothes, changed into sackcloth, and went to the Eternal's house. [2]He sent Eliakim, the palace administrator, along with Shebna, the royal secretary and some senior priests—who were also covered in sackcloth—to *fetch* Isaiah the prophet (Amoz's son).

Hezekiah's Men *(to Isaiah)*: [3]*Hezekiah is terribly upset.* The king said, "This is a *calamitous* day. It is marked by anguish, chastisement, and disgrace. *Things are as desperate for us* as for a *pregnant* woman *weakened by labor* who cannot deliver the baby because she is physically spent from the birth pangs."

[4]*Hezekiah implores you, Isaiah,* "Pray for the remnant that is left here *in Jerusalem.* Maybe the Eternal One your God will notice how blasphemous the Rabshakeh is (on orders from his master the Assyrian king) and punish them because of what the living God heard him say."

[5]When the men delivered their message as the king requested, Isaiah responded.

Isaiah: [6]*Go back to Hezekiah,* your lord *and king,* and give him these *sure* words *of confidence and hope*: The Eternal One says, "Don't let the blasphemous threats delivered by the servants of the Assyrian king make you *doubtful or* afraid. [7]Watch! I am going to *trick him,* to set a spirit against him. *Just when he is ready to attack you,* he's going to hear a rumor *that there are problems* back home *in Assyria* and he will return there. *Not only that, but* once he's back, he will die by the sword in his own land."

GRIEVE

Andrew: At the end of Isaiah 36, we read about Eliakim, Shebna, and Joah, Hezekiah's administrators, tearing their clothes upon receiving the Rabshakeh's defiant declaration to Hezekiah. And here in chapter 37, the threat becomes personal and a reality when Hezekiah, the king of the prosperous nation of Judah—*royalty*—shreds his garments, takes up residence in a sacred place, and requests his trusted friend, the prophet Isaiah, to pray on his behalf (vv. 1–4).

In ancient Jewish culture, tearing your garments symbolized bereavement, a process of mourning the death of a loved one (see *To Grieve* from chapter 5). And in the list of questions that death prompts, this tradition was an act of surrender, a tangible expression of hope in a life after, and greater than, death.

Now with the news of impending destruction and an incalculable death toll, Hezekiah shreds his clothes. He acknowledges his losses. He takes the time to process his grief. And because he recognizes rather than ignores his losses, in a move that could easily be perceived as weak and counterintuitive, the king's clothes-rending, I contend, exhibits great faith and painstaking surrender.

Judah's king is inwardly and outwardly affected by Sennacherib's stubborn threats against his lordship. And here in chapter 37, Hezekiah is not going to pretend otherwise. He is "terribly distressed." Like us, the king is human. In the midnight of his fear, as in the darkness of our circumstances, he is grieving.

ASK

Andrew: Hezekiah's willingness to grieve is the first sign that he is sensitive to a broader story composed by a sovereign God. Our second sign of the king's spiritual humility is when he asks his administration to request that Isaiah beseech God on his behalf.

In the New King James Version, Hezekiah explains his bewilderment over his current circumstances like this: "This day is a day of trouble . . . for the children have come to birth, but there is no strength to bring them forth. . . . Therefore lift up your prayer for the remnant that is left" (vv. 3–4). There is tension in his tone. Hezekiah doesn't request the latest self-help techniques or ask his allies to affirm his kingship. Instead, in his lack of understanding, he humbles himself in spiritual abandon and asks a friend to seek God with the words his apprehensive spirit cannot now formulate.

Ginny: As a private person in the truest sense, far more goes on in my life (and in my brain) than those around me will ever know. Yet I have learned through several dark seasons to fearlessly and unapologetically solicit the prayers of others. During the months following a difficult breakup (see The Pouring Out from chapter 2), I was consistently on my knees, but struggled to find God or to know what to say to Him.

I was shattered by the loss of the relationship and guilt-ridden for having let it go on so long. I understood consequences and was aware that I had brought the pain on myself, so I wasn't sure it was fair to ask God to take it away. But I also didn't have the strength or will to see the pain through if He didn't intervene somehow. My options were to either be completely miserable as I worked life out alone or to let friends and family carry me until I could walk again. In desperation, I chose the latter.

During this heartbreak period, Scott and Kim, good friends of mine who lived several hours away, frequently enlisted my help in leading worship at their church. I'm not sure if they ever knew the extent of my grief or the power of these getaways. A couple weekends a month, they would load up their two elementary-school aged kids and drive to Nashville to fetch me. After being hospitable hosts for thirty-six hours, they sacrificed their Sabbath evenings to deliver me back home. Within the four walls of their home and acceptance of their church community, I witnessed and experienced God's love and care and, even if just for a couple days, left behind the cares of my past year.

I also remember how my dear friend Dea would pray with me, sometimes for hours at a time. I was always moved by and thankful for how she articulated to God requests I didn't have the words to formulate, and how through prayer she reminded me of His promises, promises I was too tired to remember on my own. Through that season, not only did I learn how desperately I needed community, but as I experienced its healing effects, I began to believe in prayer all over again.

Andrew: In reconciling myself to the God of the Old Testament, it is has been important to recognize the areas in which the Old Testament directly correlates and foreshadows the ideals of Jesus in the New Testament. When studying Jesus' life and impact in the New Testament, it is easy to summarize much of His ministry by His relationships with others. During His ministry on earth, Jesus—the Ultimate Prophet, the Son of God—prizes human relationship. To motivate and build His kingdom, Jesus relies on the ministry of others. It seems that, for the spread of Christianity and the expansion of the New Testament church, God used and depended on the dependence of us on each other. Whew!

Throughout the Old Testament scriptures, prophets great and small comfort, admonish, guide, and magnify God's direction for the Jews. I sometimes forget that these prophets are just humans, everyday people.

Dea's prayers helped restore Ginny's faith in God's concern for her life when her heart pangs were the heaviest. A family's willingness to provide a weekend taxi carved a new space inside her worn-out soul and filled it with hope. If God's timeline is dotted with His selection of ordinary folks to deliver extraordinary declarations, perhaps we, too, like Isaiah and Ginny's friends, can be prophets for the people in our lives during their times of duress.

When Chris and Kerry were in the trenches of their relationship ordeals, Chris and I spent the better part of two weeks in late-night phone conversations. Though I lacked a parallel experience or any real insight for his painful quandaries, I could listen. And by simply being present, thinking through all sides of the equation with him, and pining with him where appropriate, over time calmed and clarified his heart—and perhaps God's heart—on the matter. Like Hezekiah and his administrative trio, like Dea and Ginny, I donned the sackcloth with my grieving brother, entered the sacred space of those late-night conversations, and gladly fulfilled Chris's request to pray to the God he wasn't even sure cared for him, or that *he* cared for, with words his lips simply could not yet recite.

When I was trekking through Wyoming with my heart on my sleeve, two acquaintances from my childhood church found me. I didn't have cell service, WiFi, or any easy way to be in touch, but Helen and Leon Short (two friends from Ash Creek Baptist Church, my birthplace congregation in Azle, Texas) were crisscrossing the northwestern United States that summer and decided to track me down. As chance, or perhaps providence, would have it, they found me just outside the east entrance of Yellowstone National Park at Pahaska Tepee Lodge—thirteen hundred miles away from home.

As we shared a meal at the lodge's restaurant, they told me that their community group from Ash Creek convened every Saturday morning to pray. And every Saturday morning they prayed for me by name. *By name.* Can you imagine how I felt to know that a group of folks, many of whom I didn't know personally, invested a portion of their weekend to implore the Creator of the universe for protection, wisdom, clarity, and love on my behalf?

I pilgrimaged seventeen hundred miles away from my home in Nashville to try to find God. One visit from Helen and Leon Short, and He found me.

Late-night conversations with my brother; lunch with hometown friends; a righteous king promised provision by a prophet: from my study and experience, God is not passively waiting from a distance for us to stumble upon Him. He is proactively seeking relationship with us. And in our darkest moments, He uses others to remind us that He sees, He knows, and He cares.

LAYING IT DOWN: PRAYER AND ORDER OF LOVE

READ ISAIAH 37:8–29.

[8]Meanwhile, the Rabshakeh learned that Sennacherib had left Lachish and was already engaged in battle against *the city of* Libnah. [9]Now the Assyrian king heard that Tirhakah, the king of Cush, *had allied himself with the Judeans and* was coming to fight against him. The news prompted him to send messengers to Hezekiah with another message.

Rabshakeh: [10]Tell the Judean king, Hezekiah, "Don't listen to your God, whom you're counting on, when He tells you that the king of Assyria won't conquer Jerusalem. [11]Look around you, and listen to the reports of what the Assyrian king has already done to the *neighboring* nations. How can he destroy them and let you get away? [12]This line of Assyrian kings has demolished *all sorts of nations and peoples. Think of* Gozan, Haran, Rezeph, and the children of Eden in Telassar. None of their gods saved them. [13]*While we're at it,* what do you think happened to the kings of Hamath, Arpad, Sepharvaim, Hena, and Ivvah? *We destroyed them. You'll not get away.*"

[14]When Hezekiah got the written message, he read it. Then he took it to the temple, spread it out before the Eternal One, [15]and began to pray.

Hezekiah: [16]Eternal, Commander of *heavenly* armies, who sits enthroned above the winged guardians—You alone are God. Only *You are supreme* over all the *nations and* kingdoms of the earth. And only You have made the heavens *above*, the earth *below, and everything in them.* [17]Please, *please* listen, Eternal One. Attend to us *here and now*; look and listen. Hear all that Sennacherib said, and all that he wrote, to ridicule *You*, the living God. [18]Eternal One, he's right about how the Assyrian kings have destroyed other nations and taken over their lands. [19]And *sure*, they ruined the gods of those nations, *smashed and* burned them. But those were not *real* gods, only the product of human hands, shaped of stone and wood. That is why they could be destroyed. [20]I implore You, Eternal One our God, help us. Save us from the *onslaught of* these Assyrians. Make it clear to the whole world that You alone are the Eternal One, that You *alone* are God.

[21-22]And Hezekiah got a response. The prophet Isaiah, Amoz's son, relayed this to him:

Isaiah: The Eternal, Israel's God, the God to whom you prayed concerning the Assyrian king, has this to say against Sennacherib:

> **Eternal One:** The virgin daughter of Zion, *lovely lady that*
> *she is,* despises you, mocks you.
> The daughter of Jerusalem tosses her head and rejects
> you.
> [23]*After all,* who is the one you've taunted and insulted?
> *Who is the one you've slandered with untruths, ugly*
> *and dismissive?*
> Who is the one you shouted at and looked down upon
> with your arrogant eyes?
> None other than the Holy One of Israel!
> [24]By way of your servants' mouths, you have blasphemed
> my Lord.

Foolish, foolish Sennacherib. You have boasted,
'My impressive company of chariots has taken me up the
        highest mountains,
    into the far reaches of the Lebanese forests.
I *myself* felled its greatest cedars, cut down the best of its
        cypresses.
    I have been to its highest peak, and claimed its thick-
        est forest.
25I have dug wells *wherever I wished,* and drunk *my fill*
        of others' water.
    I have dried up Egypt's waterways simply by walk-
        ing them.'
26*Ah, Sennacherib,* haven't you heard, *don't you know*
        that long before *you arrived,*
    way back in ancient days, I determined all of this?
I charted this course long ago, and now I bring it to pass.
    This is the reason why you turn well-fortified cities
        into heaps of rubble.
27Their hapless citizens *look on,*
    helpless, shocked, and ashamed.
They were *temporary and fragile* like grass in the field
    or tender new growth, like grass sprouting on rooftops
Blasted by a burning wind before it can grow and
    become strong.
28I know *everything about you:* where you sit, when you
        come, where you go.
    And I know your agitation against Me.
29Because of this agitation,
    and because your smug sense of security has reached
        My ears,
I will put My hook in your nose and My bit in your mouth,
    and turn you back on the road you came from.

PRAY

Andrew: The news of a growing alliance with Judah against Assyria prompts Sennacherib to dispatch his hatchet man with yet another threat for Hezekiah, veiled in language of manipulative caution (v. 11). The scheming heart of the narcissist king's message to Judah is essentially, "Give it up, sweet king. You're a goner."

But Sennacherib's string of threats belies a hairline insecurity in his seemingly impenetrable ego. *What if Judah's god is the true God? What if Hezekiah's quiet tenacity indicates a God who is in control? Is he immune to our bullying?* And his perceived fears are issued as reality when Isaiah proclaims a message of "confidence and hope" for Judah in verses 6 and 7 ("I am going to . . . set a spirit against him").

Like me, like you, Hezekiah is human through and through. Even in the light of Isaiah's prophetic promise, in the aftermath of good news, Hezekiah almost seems to validate Sennacherib's obnoxious threats with his apprehension. On paper, his fears make zero sense. But in reality, I get it. I know the feeling. And in Hezekiah's anxiety, in spite of prophetic assurances, I am relieved because it proves that I am not alone. My own fear is merely another fiber in the thread of distrust expressed among humans in spite of tested spiritual promise throughout history.

When Thomas, one of Jesus' original twelve disciples, doubts Jesus' resurrection even after his fellow disciples share their firsthand encounters with the living Messiah (John 20:24–29), his lapse of faith mirrors Hezekiah's fear of Sennacherib's threats, in spite of Isaiah's providential declaration, and the inclinations of doubt and cynicism that have pervaded humanity's spiritual beliefs throughout history.

Hezekiah is a seeker, though. Yes, he is torn between human fear and spiritual hope. But he tests out faith in God. He dips his toe in the shallow end. Instead of turning his back on a God who seems to have abandoned him, the king—through the exercise of faith—presses further in to the only one who has even a remote possibility of quelling the questions plaguing his anxiety-riddled mind. Verse 14 says, "When Hezekiah got the written message, he read it. Then he took it to the temple" and "spread it out before the Eternal One." And in faith, Hezekiah "began to pray" (v. 15).

Hezekiah's prayer reads like this: "O LORD of hosts, God of Israel, the One who dwells between the cherubim, You are God, You alone, of all the kingdoms of the earth. You have made heaven and earth. Incline Your ear, O LORD, and hear; open Your eyes, O LORD, and see; and hear all the words of Sennacherib, which he has sent to reproach the living God" (vv. 16–17 NKJV).

Hezekiah petitions. Implores. Solicits. Appeals. Communes with the *Eternal* One, the One whose knowledge is not limited by what is right in front of Hezekiah's face but imbued with infinite understanding. His prayer is not a handy resolve, but faith in action. Hezekiah recognizes his doubt, he honors the truth in Sennacherib's message (Assyria has indeed humiliated Judah's neighbors devastatingly), and he reaffirms who he believes God to be. And he prays.

ORDER OF LOVE

Andrew: I don't know what your experience with God has been. Perhaps, like some of my friends who grew up in legalistic religious traditions, your relationship with God has been stunted by some didactic god-profile bestowed upon you as a child by some supervising Sunday School literature. Or maybe your view of God was filtered through your parents, who in an effort to establish some control at home exercised "God's law" to intimidate you into submission. Or maybe you slipped up one time—*one time*—and ended up with a record. Or a pregnancy. Now every conversation carries judgment. Each glance, criticism. And the heavy circumstances of the past desecrate any opportunity of feeling worthy or loved by God, or anyone else, in the present.

I have heard these stories spill from the lips of friends who are now parents, good parents, wanting to set an example for their children, however imperfectly, of a gospel centered on a Creator who says they are worthy simply because they are alive. They want their kids to have the opportunity they never received growing up: to discover God rather than have Him dictated to them.

I grew up in a generous household. My parents raised my brothers and me with open hearts. During Sunday lunch, they would ask us what we thought about that morning's sermon. I truly felt like I possessed an important contributing voice in our family, even at a young age.

As an adult, I have asked my dad if he had any definitive advice for raising kids, since we always loved each other, generally liked each other, turned out fairly stable in life—even with our individual issues—and actively seek to relate to the Eternal. He coolly replied, "Not really." Comforting, Dad. Thanks. But he did explain that, before we were born, he and my mother surrendered to God their understanding of how to perfectly parent us. Then they did the best they humanly knew how to guide and love—not control—us along the way.

As you can imagine, this gracious way of relating to each other positively influenced my image of and relationship with God. Ironically, I still live like many of my friends who were wounded by religious legalism. I still believe that my past dictates my present, that God is a

My own fear is merely another fiber in the thread of distrust expressed among humans in spite of tested spiritual promise throughout history.

one-for-one ruler and secretly keeps score with my eternal peace in the balance.

As my friends wrestle, question, and research their way through legalism into faith, their consistent concern in Scripture is how the God of the Old Testament is congruous with the God of the New Testament. *The same God who walls up the sea to architect a dry escape for the Israelites from Egyptian slavery in Exodus also sanctions the elimination of a group of Midianites and human booty in Numbers 31? The same Creator who destroys His handiwork with a single monsoon also incarnates Himself as the rescuer of all mankind?*

Yep, it's confusing. I am asking the same questions. Stories throughout Scripture don't always make clear sense. My friends will spend a lifetime distancing themselves from the always-condemning God they feared as children so they can reconcile themselves with the God who shows up in the faces of their children around the dinner table and the caress of their wife at night. I think God can handle that.

I don't have a black and white sketch of God. I don't possess some special insight into the mind of Yahweh. I have no explanation for Scripture that remains unexplainable. I didn't create time and space. I didn't place the ability to think and reason in the mind, or the capacity to love in the heart. I have no idea how to label, much less create and organize, the atoms of the earth and body. In fact, when it comes to my experience with myself, I don't have a lot of faith in "me." So I empathize with King Hezekiah. And in the spirit of discovery, not dictation, let me offer up a possibility.

When perplexed to the max, I want to relax my thoughts inside the perspective of something—someone—with more aptitude to understand, think it through, and carry it out. In God's declarative soliloquy in verses 22–29, the divine Father expresses His exhaustion with Sennacherib and restores order by reminding the maniacal

Assyrian king that *He* is the Creator. *He* will set the scene straight. The Eternal (what a perfect name for Him in this passage) will make sense of everything.

Think about it: our entire cosmos is structured. At our very core, we correlate order with care and love. We organize our wedding days to a tee in an expression of magnificent care for our lifelong partner and close witnesses. We send our kids to school all day so their cognitive and social possibilities are endless. We work eight, ten, twelve hours a day to ensure that there is food on the table and a roof over our heads. We take out the trash for our spouses so the house won't stink and our love life won't suffer. We plan meals and rides and acoustic tunes for the older folks in our community who are having trouble caring for themselves. Order is at the heart of our concern for each other. Attention to detail says, "I love you."

Because of how my friends' legalistic experiences growing up have affected their views of God, especially through an Old Testament lens, I have a newfound sensitivity to Scripture passages where God renders immediate justice on those who are infringing on the rights of His people. By modern definition, defending the defenseless is termed "social justice." Caring for those in need is trendy. Yet when divine justice peeks its head over the horizon to protect those whom God loves at all costs, we cower in cynicism.

Dictionary.com defines "compassion" as "a feeling of deep sympathy and sorrow for another who is stricken by misfortune, accompanied by a strong desire to alleviate the suffering."[4] The prophet Isaiah describes the Suffering Servant (who is Jesus, God's solution to this human mess) as "grief's patient friend" (Isaiah 53:3). God's listening ear and call to order in Isaiah 37 exhibit complete compassion. The people of Judah have been actively seeking relationship with God through service to Him, and yet they are being ambushed by self-satisfying, land-hungry neighbors. As they are approached with this injustice and surrender the ensuing anxiety in prayer, the Eternal, because of His justice-rendering love, stands ready to alleviate their suffering by taking it all back to square one.

I am convinced that in our day-to-day doings, as in Hezekiah's ancient appeal, God is restoring order. For my friends, for their children, yes, even for me, He will protect us at *any* cost. In spite of my finite misunderstandings, I will continually spend my days discovering who this infinitely compassionate Creator really is.

NOT YET NORMAL: FINDING HOME

READ ISAIAH 37:30–32.

Eternal One *(to Hezekiah)*: [30]Here is a sign for you: *you'll know it's true by seeing that in three years, life will be normal again*: This year you'll live off of what grows spontaneously. Next year, you'll live off of what grows from that. In the third year, you'll do the planting and harvesting—fields and vineyards—and eat from what grows. [31]And those who have survived in this land of Judah—this remnant—will strengthen their roots and become productive again.

> [32]A small group of survivors will emerge from Jerusalem,
>   from Zion, the mountain *of God's choosing.*

Isaiah: The intensive passion of the Eternal, Commander of *heavenly* armies, will drive this to completion.

FINDING HOME

Andrew: I have never received the benefit of an audible conversation with God. Though I make an effort to connect with Him one-on-one through prayer, most of how I relate to God is through my story and the stories of others, including those in Scripture. But in this postlude to chapter 37, God speaks clearly and directly to Hezekiah. He doesn't use the prophetic channels of Isaiah or Hezekiah's administrative trio. He doesn't conjure up mysterious signs and signals. Instead, Hezekiah's Creator speaks a promise of restoration to His creation, "In three years, life will be normal again" (v. 30).

Normal. Way to go, Hezekiah. I have waited my entire adult life to hear that one word focus a spiritual promise. My experience? Life is not normal. Confusing? Complex? Abnormal? Yes. But far from normal. I have a hunch you can relate.

But even in the driest of spiritual dry spells, streams meander through the desert. An unexpected sign of life gifts us with thirst-quenching insights into the unknowable.

I was given a key to an uninsulated lodge in the middle of Wyoming's dramatically changing climate with a perfectly playable 1930s piano inside. Wading through conflicting and often overwhelming emotions thousands of miles away from home, each time my fingertips pressed those yellowed ivories on that old upright, I felt normal.

Chris and Kerry, un-engaged and living a couple hours away from each other, would meet at a restaurant in the middle, and on neutral ground begin dating again. And for one evening, the confused couple felt normal.

In the middle of my sister-in-law's chemotherapy, Trey and Stephanie would take advantage of the brief window when Steph was feeling her best, order pizza, cover the living room floor with blankets, fire up a Disney flick, and snuggle with the cutest toddler girls in East Texas. And for two unobstructed hours, a princess movie made them feel normal.

"*In three years life will be normal again*" (v. 30). When Granddad made that mysterious passage from one life to the next, my mom felt the sobering transition from being a daughter to becoming a matriarch. For a brief period, she was displaced, out of sync. With death comes a lot of *not* normal. When we grieve, our hearts' sneaking suspicion is that death was not God's original design for life.

In the midnight of our confusions, I want to adopt Hezekiah's posture of surrender. I want to lay down my life, not just my circumstances, and begin to discover God all over again—not simply as my disciplining Father, but as a compassionate friend.

Perhaps God's "intensive passion" to drive Hezekiah's circumstances to completion is a glimpse of the paradigm shift to come, a glimpse into the fervor of God's desire to restore the entire cosmos, to reorient everything right, out of His love for everyone.

CAN GOD CHANGE HIS MIND?

READ ISAIAH 38:1–4.

Meanwhile, *back in Judah,* Hezekiah became very sick and was about to die. *Learning of it,* Isaiah, Amoz's son, went to visit him.

Isaiah: Here is what the Eternal One has to say:

Eternal One: Get your affairs in order. You are going to die. You are not going to recover from this.

²Hezekiah turned his face to the wall and started praying.

Hezekiah: ³Eternal One, I beg you to remember how I have followed the path You set before me, and how I did so with all my heart. Remember how I have done what You wanted *with sincerity of purpose every step of the way.*

Then Hezekiah *broke down and* wept. He wept and wept. ⁴Then a *different* word from the Eternal came upon *the prophet* Isaiah.

Our leader and University Minister at the time, Matt Kerlin, was constantly presenting our teenage theology with thoughtful challenges. One Sunday, he asked us to think about the sovereignty of God. By asking us to ponder God's supremacy, Matt was trying to help us dream of a God who is alive and involved in the details.

Perhaps, he posed, rather than dictating our every move, God is creating time as it happens. Literally. "What if," he asked, "God is bringing the sun up every morning, and setting it to rest every night?" After all, an entity is not truly omnipotent if he cannot also exercise restraint. He cannot be all-powerful if he cannot also control his own power.

My mind was blown. Having grown up in rural Texas in a family who explored and dialogued about the many dimensions of God's character, I was immediately drawn to the possibility that God is not simply a divine manipulator, watching it all play out in the hunger games[5] of God, but that He, in fact, deeply cares. And as these Old Testament stories suggest, He is involved in the details.

God's famous promise to the Israelites through Solomon in 2 Chronicles 7:14 suggests that the Creator of the cosmos is concerned about every person's request: "If My people who are called by My name will humble themselves, and pray and seek My face, and turn from their wicked ways, then I will hear from heaven, and will forgive their sin and heal their land" (NKJV). When Hezekiah entered the temple to seek a response from God concerning Assyria's threats, he asked God to "incline" His ear (Isa. 37:17 NKJV). To bend low. To listen closely.

Isaiah 38 raises the question, *Can our requests prompt a change of heart in the Almighty?* This is a fearful question among legalists who promote the dogma that God cannot be both the great I Am and also the gentle shepherd, but for those living with the heartbeat of grace these queries are imaginative and hopeful, a blueprint for all of Scripture and our life experiences. The mystery of God should be relished in the hearts of disciples across time and space.

Q&A:
Prayer Perspectives

Ginny: How has prayer affected your perspective or circumstances?

Andrew: I am not a good prayer person. Perhaps through more experience and with deeper trust I will pray without ceasing. Though my prayer closet is rarely occupied, I do like to have walking conversations with God, an ongoing experience when I remember to recognize what I believe to be His presence in everyday goings-on. While walking through an extended dark night of the soul a few years ago in Wyoming, I woke up every day and said out loud, "Good morning, God." I just wanted to exercise a small step of faith in a period otherwise plagued with doubt. Over time, I could tangibly feel the friendship of God. I'm not talking about feelings-driven spirituality. I am talking about the natural effects of the inner spiritual discipline of prayer. My perspectives experience significant shifts when I talk with God. Depression may not immediately subside, but it does begin to give way to joy and hope. Anxiety steadily transitions to peace. Jealousy and discontentment focus instead on the value of others and inspire gratefulness for my own life and opportunities. My entire environment, even nature itself, seems to bend in a posture of worship when I pray.

QUESTIONS for Reflection

1. Why did the king tear his clothes, put on sackcloth (like burlap), and go into the temple? What does this reveal about his internal turmoil? About his faith?

2. When have you endured deep grief or fear? How did you respond?

3. In your experiences with grief and fear, who has provided help, comfort, or guidance? How has God used other people in your life to help you through difficult times?

4. God tells Sennacherib that He deliberately orchestrated all the events that are unfolding (v. 26). Why? What does this tell you about God? About the deeds of human beings?

5. What events in your own life has God deliberately orchestrated? How can this insight help you to endure times of suffering and hardship?

HYMN FOR LEAVING

(Words and Music: Andrew Greer and Ben Rosenbush)

Leave behind
Everything we've known
Each goodbye
Aches within our soul
Hallelujah
Lujah
Falling hard
Long away from home
Distant call
Soothes the wounds we hold
Hallelujah
Lujah
Knees are dirty
Hands are trembling
Hearts are beating fast
Tears are falling
Arms are reaching
Through the time we had
Had we known
Leaving was part of the giving
Then our hearts
Would ache less
For the missing You
Hallelujah
Lujah

CHAPTER 8

WITHOUT YOU

> "I couldn't hear You whispering to me above all of the noise / But now as You hold me, the world fades away / And I'm changed by Your beautiful voice ..."
>
> —Ginny Owens, "Without You"

> "The grace of God means something like: Here is your life. You might never have been, but you are because the party wouldn't have been complete without you. Here is the world. Beautiful and terrible things will happen. Don't be afraid. I am with you. Nothing can ever separate us."
>
> —Frederick Buechner, *Wishful Thinking* [1]

> "God has never kicked the world to pieces. He keeps reentering the world, keeps offering himself to the world—by grace, keeps somehow blessing the world, making possible a kind of life which we all, in our deepest being, hunger for."
>
> —Frederick Buechner [2]

Ginny: "Doctor Steve" and I first met on a Sunday morning during a band rehearsal at church. I had just joined the worship and arts staff at a large church in Franklin, Tennessee, a thriving suburb just south of Nashville, and Steve was one of the acoustic guitar players. At first, settling in to my new church home was overwhelming. With so many new names, voices, songs, and protocols to learn, I mostly felt like an outsider. Steve and I, however, became friends right away.

Always kind and positive, Steve's cheerful disposition makes him a delightful asset to the team, especially during break-of-dawn rehearsals. He is also humble. After three years of being friends, he finally divulged that, in addition to serving elementary students as a speech pathologist, he is a full-time college professor with a PhD. Hence, I address him as "Doctor." (Who keeps that kind of information under wraps?)

Steve, Kristy, and their Branson brood look like a typical all-American family. Their three kids have hip names: Shiloh (8), Sydney (5), and Fender (3)—and inhabit every room with vigorous energy. Kristy is an ER nurse, working only a couple days each week so she can be at home with the kids. When Steve is not conducting speech therapy or lecturing college students, he is refereeing family fun or teaching Shiloh to play guitar. This hardworking couple juggles more life in a day than most people think about tasking in a month, and yet they always appear calm and at peace with the process.

As we wrapped the worship service one Sunday morning, Steve told me the unbelievable story that forever changed the trajectory of his family's life. Still the new girl on the block, I was wrestling with a slew of doubts and insecurities that morning. After hearing Steve and Kristy's story, I left moved and humbled by their profound journey of surrender.

"Kristy and I have been on an adventure since day one," Steve says, laughing as he reminisces. "We met in one of the seediest bars in Columbia, Missouri. From the first moment, I knew there was something special about her." Steve lived in Nashville; Kristy lived in Columbia, Missouri. And after two years of long-distance dating, they married and began a new life together in Nashville. A year later, the Bransons found out they were expecting their first child. "My best-laid plans were coming true," says Kristy. "Married at twenty-three. First baby by twenty-five."

Around the same time, a friend of Steve's who attends our church invited the Bransons to come hear him play guitar in the worship band. Kristy grew up in the Catholic church; Steve grew up in a tiny Baptist church. By the time they were married, both profess that they believed in Christ's saving power, but neither was pursuing a spiritual life. Moved by the music and message that weekend, they became regular attenders. That was nine years ago; they have been involved ever since.

A few months into their new church life, Shiloh Branson was born. First-time parents Kristy and Steve were overjoyed with the birth of their baby girl, but completely overwhelmed with the process of taking care of her. Shiloh never ate more than an ounce of food before gagging, coughed often, shook her head violently, perspired profusely, and cried constantly. The only way to calm her down was to keep her moving. They were continuously on-call until they discovered the infamous, life-changing bouncy chair. "Even at night," Steve remembers, "we kept the bouncy chair beside our bed so Kristy and I could take turns keeping it in motion with our feet."

"If Shiloh had been our second child," Kristy says, "we would have known something wasn't right. But doctors just assumed our girl was predisposed to terrible bouts of colic and an unusually diffi-cult temperament." For the young couple, the trial was heavy. "We were learning a whole new level of patience," Steve admits. "It was difficult to be around our friends whose kids didn't cry as often or need constant attention."

Hoping for a mini-vacation during the last week of Kristy's maternity leave, the new family headed to her stomping grounds in Missouri. Shiloh, now four months old, was so miserable they repeatedly pulled

After hearing Steve and Kristy's story, I left moved and humbled by their profound journey of surrender.

the car over to calm her down. By the time they arrived at Kristy's parents' house, Shiloh had grown so agitated that she wouldn't eat. Kristy consulted her pediatrician, and heeded his advice to take her little girl to the emergency room. After forty-five minutes of screaming, Shiloh went limp and nearly stopped breathing.

"The doctor finally came in to report that, after reviewing the X-rays, it was clear that Shiloh was experiencing heart failure," Kristy recounts, fighting back tears still eight years later. "I was shocked. Speechless. I thought my little girl was going to die."

Shiloh needed immediate advanced medical attention and with hazardous winter weather grounding all of St. Louis's medevac helicopters, she was painstakingly transported to St. Louis Children's Hospital by ambulance while her parents and grandparents followed. It was the longest two hours of their lives.

When they arrived, the doctor's diagnosis was unnerving. "Your little girl is one of the sickest babies we've ever seen. We don't know whether she'll make it through the night."

For the next ten days, the Bransons lived in the hospital waiting room, praying for a miracle and trying to comprehend the unknown. As the news spread about Shiloh's condition, family, friends, and even strangers from around the world also prayed.

Shiloh was eventually diagnosed with dilated cardiomyopathy—a condition where the heart becomes enlarged and too weak to pump blood appropriately. She rallied on medication, allowing the vulnerable girl enough flexibility to be transported by LifeFlight home to Nashville's Vanderbilt Hospital where cardiologists would organize an ongoing treatment plan.

"We have little control over what will happen today or tomorrow. We have no choice but to rely on God for everything."

They were encouraged by Shiloh's renewed strength, but when Kristy arrived, she received more devastating news. Shiloh's ejection fraction, her heart's pumping percentage, was only 8 percent. Her heart should have been pumping at 70 percent. The grieving parents were given the devastating news: their baby would need a heart transplant to survive.

As an ER nurse, Kristy was especially discouraged by the transplant option. Her experience had shown that transplant patients were always sickly and had an overall poor quality of life. Yet it was Shiloh's only option for life.

Five weeks after Shiloh was placed on the transplant waiting list, Steve was watching the local news in the waiting room. A horrifying story about a little boy who had been violently abused by his mother's boyfriend disrupted his attention, and his emotions gave way. "I didn't understand how anyone could do such terrible things to a child," Steve says. "It seemed so unfair, especially while our little girl was so sick just down the hall."

Early the next morning, Kristy and Steve finally received the call. A heart had been found for Shiloh. As they would later learn, that heart belonged to the boy from the previous night's newscast. At seven p.m. on March 13, 2007, doctors performed a five-hour surgery to replace Shiloh's defective heart.

"It was two a.m. before the doctors let us see our baby again," says Kristy. "She was connected to IVs, tubes, and wires, and there was a huge incision the length of her chest. I nearly passed out when I saw her. It just made it all so real. Surgeons had replaced our baby's heart with someone else's heart. That's not something you ever dream you will face as a parent."

Two-and-a-half weeks later, all three Bransons went home. The months that followed were nerve-racking. Shiloh was given thirteen different medicines every day in addition to multiple hospital visits each week. Some medications had to be administered three times a day. She frequently worked herself into such a frenzy that the first dose would not stay down and would have to be readministered. "We learned to give her one medication, wait fifteen minutes, give the next one, and repeat until they were all done," Kristy remembers. "A few hours later, we would repeat the process. It was a full-time job."

Shiloh has never known life without medicine, doctor visits, or her special heart. Much more than a muscle beating inside her chest, Shiloh's heart exudes love for others. Vivacious and energetic, she has never met a person who remained a stranger. Since she was a toddler, she has been easily moved to tears by beautiful melodies and sad stories. She loves taking charge of her younger siblings. And more than anything, she loves Jesus and loves to talk about Him with everyone. Shiloh's preschool teacher told Kristy that she overheard Shiloh comforting a peer who was crying by telling her, "You don't have to be sad. Just ask Jesus to come and help you, and He will always be right there with you. He is always here with me too."

"I like to think that part of Shiloh's purpose for being here is to bring light and hope to others, encouraging them with the good news of Jesus," Kristy muses. "Her passion is inspiring, even for us as her parents."

Facing the unknown is a constant reality for the Bransons. Statistics show that a heart like Shiloh's could perform normally for up to nineteen years before another transplant is required. Her anti-rejection medications weaken the immune system and increase her chances of illness. Even a little head cold means a trip to the hospital. So far, Shiloh has managed beautifully and stayed mostly healthy, but her parents are constantly aware of what could happen. "She talks to me about heaven and how when she gets there she will find the little boy whose heart she has and give him a huge hug for saving her life," Steve tells. "I am in awe. It is a miracle that my little girl is alive, and a true miracle that so early in her life she is captivated by heaven and Christ's love."

Shiloh's story, and the person she has become, has had a profound impact on her family and her community. "I would never wish our experience on anyone," Steve admits, "but the outcome, I would wish for everyone. We are not the people we once were. Our journey of faith is real and deep."

Kristy echoes the sentiment. "We have little control over what will happen today or tomorrow. We have no choice but to rely on God for everything."

THE DISRUPTIVE WHISPERS OF HOLINESS: REMOVE AND RESTORE

READ 2 CHRONICLES 34:1–13.

Josiah was 8 years old when he became king, and he reigned 31 years in Jerusalem. [2]He *was one of the few great kings of Israel, who* determinedly obeyed the Eternal and followed the example of his ancestor David. [3-4]His zeal for the True God of David began in the 8th year of his reign while he was still a child *of 16*, but he did not begin his reforms of Judah and Jerusalem until he was 20 years old. Then he removed the high places, chopped down the sacrificial altars and incense altars of the Baals, and smashed the carved and molten images of Asherah and other gods. He then took the broken pieces of the icons, crushed them into powder, and sprinkled that powder on the graves of the people who had worshiped them. [5]He even burned the bones of the priests *who had served those gods* on the cultic altars to completely purge Judah and Jerusalem. [6]He then continued *his reforms* throughout the region, including Manasseh, Ephraim, Simeon, and Naphtali and their surrounding villages, [7]where he *personally* smashed the carved images of Asherah and other gods into powder and chopped down the incense altars. Then he returned to Jerusalem.

⁸By the 18th year of his reign, Josiah had cleansed the nation and the temple. *Now it was time to repair them both by rebuilding the temple.* He sent Shaphan (son of Azaliah), Maaseiah (a city official), and Joah (son of Joahaz the recorder) to the temple of the True God, the Eternal, in order to organize repairs there. ⁹*First,* they took the money *from the temple coffers* and gave it to Hilkiah, the high priest, *so he could oversee the funds for the temple repairs.* The money had been collected at the temple by the Levite doorkeepers from those remaining in the Northern Kingdom, including Manasseh and Ephraim, and from all those in *the Southern Kingdom, including* Judah, Benjamin, and the city of Jerusalem. ¹⁰The money went to the Eternal's temple construction supervisors who then subcontracted the work to tradesmen and craftsmen. ¹¹Those subcontractors purchased cut stone, timber, and couplings to rebuild the portions of the temple that had become ruined because of the neglect by the kings of Judah. ¹²The subcontractors were dependable workers, following the guidance of their supervisors: Jahath and Obadiah (Levites from the clan of Merari), Zechariah and Meshullam (*Levites* from the clan of Kohath), and the Levite musicians. ¹³These supervisors guided everyone on the job, *from the subcontractors and foremen* to the unskilled laborers, while performing their regular duties of record keepers, officials, and gatekeepers.

REMOVE

Ginny: In 2 Chronicles 34, we learn of another child whose special heart had a profound impact on his surrounding community. A little background: Josiah began his thirty-one-year reign over Judah at just eight years old, after his father Amon, who ruled in defiance of God, was assassinated by his own officials. Scripture records Josiah as the last monarch of Judah to revere God, and his leadership ended just before the Jews were exiled to Babylon (vv. 1–3).

Even as a boy, Josiah was passionate about the Eternal. That focused allegiance motivated him to completely purge his constituency of any obstacle to worshiping God (vv. 4–5). Considering our current cultural fear of any action remotely violent, no matter the cause, today we might find Josiah's inflamed manner of cleansing the kingdom radical. And even though Josiah has contextual excuse, since many ancient cultures were dramatically more violent than our twenty-first century Western world, deeper investigation reveals more possible reasons for his zealous actions.

First, Josiah's desecration of altars and the burning of priests' bones directly fulfill a prophecy voiced to King Jeroboam (1 Kings 13:1–3), Israel's king, a couple centuries prior, who had constructed a plethora of altars and shrines in Israel's Northern Kingdom to prevent the people from going to Jerusalem (located in Judah) to worship at the temple (1 Kings 12:26–32).

Second, King Josiah, perhaps unknowingly, was following the command that God imparted to the Israelites through Moses to eliminate false gods. The destruction of idols was not only allowed, but mandated by God. ("Break down the altars, smash their sacred stones, and cut down their Asherah poles" [Ex. 34:13; Deut. 7:5 NIV].)

And from the perspective of both Jews and non-Jews of that period, the presence of anything related to the dead made a place unclean. So Josiah burned the bones and spread the ashes over the shrines to bring disgrace on the pagan sites, deterring people from returning to worship their false idols.

This God-fearing king was intent on making a radical change throughout his kingdom. Second Kings 23 says, "Neither before nor after Josiah was there a king like him who turned to the LORD as he did—with all his heart and with all his soul and with all his strength, in accordance with all the Law of Moses" (v. 25 NIV). This description of Josiah mirrors the language Jesus uses in Matthew 22 to describe the first and greatest commandment: loving God. Josiah's fire for the Eternal and his efforts to unite the kingdom in worshiping God paints a picture of the pursuit of holiness.

This 2 Kings challenge to follow the Eternal with my whole being emerges as a clear definition that is reiterated throughout the Old and New Testaments. God issues this creed to the Israelites in Deuteronomy: "Love the LORD your God with all your heart and with all your soul and with all your strength" (Deut. 6:5 NIV). And when Jesus speaks with the Pharisees during His ministry on earth, He restates these words as the ultimate command for Christian discipleship (Matt. 22:37; Luke 10:27).

When I was growing up in church, holiness was often an abstract attribute of God's character that I was exhorted to emulate through Scriptures or sermons, but a term difficult to apply. In the Old Testament, holiness is defined as "set apart." The author of Leviticus describes Israel as God's holy nation, chosen by the Eternal: "I am the LORD your God, who set you apart from the nations" (Lev. 20:24 NIV). God Himself is also holy and "set apart," possessing a perfection and majesty that is beyond humanity. (See Hannah's song in 1 Samuel 2: "No one is holy like the LORD, for there is none besides You, nor is there any rock like our God" [1 Sam. 2:2 NKJV].) And we can be made holy. God is perfect and pure, and our reflection of *His* image makes us perfect and pure, or sets us apart. ("You shall be holy; for I am holy" [Lev. 11:44 NKJV].)[3]

Today, living under the new covenant—Christ's sacrifice rather than our ethical purity—reconciles us to God and makes us holy. Surrender to Christ's work in us motivates the admonishment of the disciple Peter, "But just as he who called you is holy, so be holy in all you do" (1 Peter 1:15 NIV). As Philip Yancey poetically states, "If we

> **It was when I began to realize God's deep love for me that I was compelled to pursue Him.**

comprehend what Christ has done for us, then surely out of grati-
tude . . . we will strive for holiness, not to make God love us,
but because he already does."[4]

So if loving the Eternal with all we are and all we have is in
essence to inhabit holiness, what could this ideal look like in our
everyday lives?

Josiah pursued God in much the same way that God had been
pursuing His people since the days of Abraham—faithfully with
constant devotion and unbridled passion. In my own story, it was
when I began to realize God's deep love for me that I was compelled
to pursue Him. Though I had trusted in Jesus since age four, not until
after college did I begin to understand that God offers me more
than eternal salvation. He *loves* me more deeply than I could ever
imagine.

As this reality took root in my heart, my relationship with the
Ruler of the universe morphed into a personal companionship with
a tender, loving, heavenly Father. Not having grown up in the same
household as my dad, this newfound God-relationship opened up a
place in my heart that had been inaccessible for many years. I began
to talk to God about everything. I wanted to know how He wanted
me to handle situations. I wanted to be motivated towards what
He wanted me to pursue. More than ever before, I loved Him and
desired to follow Him. Since then, I have lived seasons when I ceased
to value most what the Eternal wanted, only to find my heart rest-
less and in constant search until I stopped to hear His whisper again.

As I pray, study Scripture, and interact with others, I hear these
disruptive whispers of His holiness. With a constant invitation to
change, they challenge me to purge second-nature habits and com-
pel me to embrace new perspectives and behaviors. As my love for
the Lord deepens, quiet urgings insist that I purge the sins and false
gods that stand between God and me. I am compelled to do the

work in our relationship—not because God won't love me if I don't, but because He loves me.

These whispers of holiness disturb my comfortable, self-managing existence and open my eyes to the dissonance of sin in my life. They pronounce my tendency to worry and be negative, bringing to light my lack of trust in God. They reveal the pitfalls of my southern niceness, begging me to replace this non-confrontational nature with an open and willing heart that, beyond being polite, beats with real compassion for others—the same heart I have discovered in God. My laundry list of prayer requests for my welfare is slowly being replaced by prayers for friends, family, people in need, and for opportunities to be useful in their lives. And as I pray, I notice His still small voice reminding me of my countless gifts and blessings.

Before Shiloh's transplant, Kristy said her desire to control her circumstances dictated her life and deterred her from real relationship with God. "Not so much anymore," she laughs. "As I press in to God, I let go of my need to control. Even when I don't like the answer He gives, I know I can trust that He will hold us through any circumstance. He has rebuilt my life completely. I am nothing like the person I was before."

RESTORE

Ginny: Josiah understands what it requires to pursue the Eternal. After a deliberate and thorough removal of the kingdom's false gods, he gets to the task of repairing the temple, deteriorating due to years of neglect. Josiah is unwavering in his quest to resurrect a house of worship for the True God. The work is accomplished in an organized, orderly manner, and everyone pitches in. Even the musicians help supervise the reconstruction. The thought of creative types overseeing manual labor reeks of danger, yet I smile when I think how everyone puts forth the effort and is used practically to rebuild the temple successfully. I am encouraged by this group pursuit of God's holiness.

As we eliminate false gods and re-center our worship on the Eternal, we need trusted community to walk with us, pray for us, and enlighten us with their own faith-building experiences. King Josiah's perseverance and the Israelites' concerted efforts encourage me to stay the course, knowing that as I pursue the Eternal through prayer, study, and connection with others, He will whisper to me of His love and what is important to Him.

DISCOVERING GOD'S WORDS: EXAMINE AND INQUIRE

READ 2 CHRONICLES 34:14–25.

[14]As Josiah's *three* servants were bringing out the money from the Eternal's treasury, Hilkiah the priest made an unexpected discovery. *Deep inside the temple storerooms, long forgotten, was* the Eternal's law book, rules He had given *to the Israelites* through Moses.

Hilkiah *(to Shaphan the scribe)*: [15]Look at what I have found. This is the Eternal's law book, which was buried inside the temple.

Hilkiah gave the book to Shaphan, [16]who took it to the king and affirmed that they were proceeding *with the temple repairs*.

Shaphan *(to Josiah)*: All the repairs you planned for the temple are going well. [17]Your *three* servants have taken the money from the Eternal's temple treasury and allocated it to the supervisors and subcontractors. *In the midst of temple restoration works,* [18]Hilkiah the priest *made a discovery.* He found this book.

Shaphan then read these laws in the presence of the king.

¹⁹When the king heard those words, *he realized how far his nation had drifted from God's path, and* he tore his clothes *in mourning.* ²⁰He then summoned *five of his high-ranking officials:* Hilkiah, Ahikam (son of Shaphan), Abdon (son of Micah), Shaphan the scribe, and Asaiah the king's servant.

Josiah: ²¹You must intercede for me and for all those who remain in Israel and Judah. *Ask the Lord* about these laws which we have just found. The Eternal must be furious with us because our ancestors disobeyed His laws in this book. Soon He will unleash that anger and punish us all.

²²The *four* men including Hilkiah went straight to Huldah the prophetess in Jerusalem's Second Quarter *because they knew He would speak through her.* Huldah was the wife of Shallum (son of Tokhath, son of Hasrah, the keeper of the wardrobe).

Huldah: ²³⁻²⁴These are the words of the Eternal God of Israel: "Tell *Josiah,* king of Judah, that I will indeed curse this nation and these people, just as the book says I will, ²⁵because they have disobeyed Me and made sacrifices to other gods intending to infuriate Me by their actions. The pain and suffering you are about to experience will be *unbearable and* unending.

EXAMINE

Ginny: In our polite, politically correct world, I am grateful for a handful of friends who are willing to communicate honestly with me what they think of my choices. Truth? If I know what kind of response I am going to get from them in a certain situation, I may avoid them temporarily. But when I finally open up, they always offer truth, insight, and encouragement that remind me I am not on this journey alone.

I have come to regard Scripture in much the same way. When I finally open it up after a period of avoidance, the inspired words of those pages always offer eye-opening, encouraging companionship. Martin Luther said of Scripture, "The Bible is alive, it speaks to me; it has feet, it runs after me; it has hands, it lays hold of me." I completely agree.

I have always been an avid reader, but I haven't spent time reading and wrestling with the mysteries of the Scriptures as I now wish I had. I have read through the four gospels and New Testament epistles numerous times, and I love extracting the verses of comfort and encouragement from the psalms. But I have always assumed that the Bible was too immense and too confusing to get too involved with.

Over the past year and a half, I have been venturing through a one-year Bible app on my phone. I'm discovering the truth of Luther's words. Not only has the Bible become for me the most fascinating book I have ever read, but it *feels* alive. In every reading, I'm amazed by something new that I uncover, and disappointed that I am just now in the uncovering process. I am gaining a better understanding of the God of the Old Testament and how desperately He loved His people. I see myself in the Old Testament narratives, realizing how often I mirror the Jews' behaviors and how often God's grace delivers me from myself. I am getting a deeper sense of what it meant for Christ to fulfill the law, and a richer understanding of His humble, vulnerable life. All that I have read so far, including Psalms, Proverbs, and the letters of the apostles, challenges me to think and live differently.

Like me, the Israelites had much to learn about God's book. Even the high priest first discovered it buried in a temple storeroom while withdrawing money from the treasury for temple repairs. The Book of the Law had been "long forgotten." Yet somehow, though he had presumably never seen the book, Hilkiah realized its importance, as did the minister of state, Shaphan, who took it immediately to King Josiah. In the king's presence, Shaphan read aloud the words of God's book in the palace for the first time in generations—not surprising when we consider the intermittent worship of the Eternal by Judah's kings (vv. 14–18).

Second Kings 22 and 23 outline Josiah's history similarly, but with more detailed descriptions of the measures he took to purge the Israelite kingdom of its false gods. The Voice Bible's introduction to 2 Kings explains that the book's authors wrote it "to remind future generations of the consequences of abandoning the instruction God provides in the law." Sounds like a foreboding, legalistic message, doesn't it? As in Josiah's day, our society is not fond of God's words and laws and, to some degree, understandably. The Bible has been misused so often that we are terrified to even investigate and explore its relevance.

Several nights ago, a good friend shared with me over dinner his passionate distaste for legalism. He grew up in a church and family where Christianity meant following an extensive set of rules, and failing to follow the rules meant an extensive set of consequences and a withholding of God's love. "I missed out on grace completely," he said. "I was fed a steady diet of what not to do. 'Don't drink. Don't dance. Don't swear.' I never heard anything about pursuing a relationship with God and discovering the beauty of who He is."

I can relate. It has always been easier for me to try to follow the rules than it has been to accept the gift of unconditional love offered me by the Eternal. But the stirrings occurring in my soul as a result of diving into Scripture leave me wondering how I ever thought I knew anything of what is important to God without it. And though many of the laws and commands in its pages perplex me, Scripture provides a deeper sense of how immeasurable is the Lord's love and forgiveness, and how desperately I am in need of it.

One particular Scripture passage brought hope and comfort to Kristy during Shiloh's transplant. "John 9 recounts the story of Jesus healing the blind man," she says. "All the people ask whether he or his parents sinned. When Shiloh was in the hospital waiting for a heart, a lady confronted Steve. She said the reason Shiloh was sick was because Steve's dad was a Mason, and God was punishing our family for it. In John 9, Jesus responded to these people by saying that it had nothing to do with the sin of the man or his parents, but instead it was so that God may be glorified through the man's testimony. The first time I read this story, I got chills and could not believe what I was reading. It brought such hope and gave me new confidence in who God is."

As Josiah hears the words God spoke through Moses, his eyes are opened to just how far his people have wandered from the path of the Eternal. The agony Josiah experiences through his fear that Israel will be destroyed because of their sin propels him to tear his clothes in overwhelming grief and hopeful repentance. But in his broken, bewildered state, he takes action (v. 19).

INQUIRE

Ginny: Josiah assembles a group of five trusted officials, including the prompting parties, Hilkiah and Shaphan. He knows that God is angry. Taking to heart the words they had read to him, he asks these men to inquire of the Eternal what will happen to Israel as a result of their years of disobedience. The men turn to a trusted source, Huldah, a prophetess and cousin to the prophet Jeremiah, for a response from the Eternal. In 2 Kings 22, Huldah does not mince words when delivering the Eternal's message to the Israelites: "I will bring calamity on this place and on its inhabitants—all the words of the book which the king of Judah has read—because they have forsaken Me and burned incense to other gods, that they might provoke me to anger with all the works of their hands.

Therefore My wrath shall be aroused against this place and shall not be quenched" (2 Kings 22:16–17 NKJV).

The Book of the Law that prompts Josiah's mourning and repentance and Huldah's critical directive is understood by most scholars to contain primary texts used by the writer of Deuteronomy. While reading Deuteronomy in my year-long Bible reading plan, I was astonished to learn how often, and for how long, the Eternal had been cautioning His people from worshiping false gods—a theme recurring throughout the three preceding books as well. As Moses leads the Hebrews out of Egypt and shepherds them during their forty-year desert walk, God warns that worshiping false gods would ultimately destroy the nation of Israel. And so Moses pleads with the people to stick with God (Deut. 29)—and now again with Josiah and Huldah: same covenant, same caution.

But God's covenant is more than a doomsday directive. God's grace is evident throughout Old Testament law. In the same Deuteronomic covenant given to Moses by God, Moses says to the Israelites, "When everything I've described to you has happened, and you've experienced *first* the blessings *of obedience* and then the curses *for disobedience,* if you reflect on these blessings and curses while you're living in the nations where the Eternal your God has scattered you; and if you and your descendants return to Him completely, heart and soul, *and listen to His voice* . . . then He will have mercy on you and bring you back from captivity" (Deut. 30:1–3).

As in this instance of discovering how long God had loved His people, I am constantly surprised by how often Scripture sheds light on His bigger picture working through my small-picture life. Sometimes I find comfort and encouragement. Sometimes I am disturbed and unsettled. I suppose that's why it is easier to leave it buried in the storeroom.

Just as when he spearheaded the temple's reconstruction, Josiah asks for help. Instead of hiding in the back room of a gilded palace, quaking in fear or resenting God and His ominous words, he seeks to understand what he finds in Scripture by reaching out to his inner circle for support. *Together*, they navigate the revelation of God through Scripture.

Andrew: The support of community in valuing and understanding Scripture has been imperative to my spiritual life. Much like dissecting elusive poetry during my high school AP English courses, I have difficulty unburying the nuggets of truth inside each meter and rhyme of Scripture. My Bible findings have proven to be life changing, whereas breaking down an Ernest Hemingway or Emily Dickinson creation, even in all their literary splendor, is enlightening at best—yet the exercise is the same. Reading Scripture is difficult. It requires study, discipline, repetition, time to think, and lots of help.

I make a frequent habit of asking friends whom I trust, as people first and as thinkers second, to discourse on a handful of cultural hot topics infiltrating the cross-section of society and church today. What is their take on what Scripture says about each topic? How do they interpret that Scripture in the day-in and day-out of their lives? How are their relationships and their lives directly affected by each topic of conversation? This dialogue around our corporate examination and inquisition of oft-debatable Scripture changes our digestion of Scripture from a check list of must-dos to a world of possibility in how to live well and connect with God even better.

God's covenant is more than a doomsday directive. God's grace is evident throughout Old Testament law.

THE EFFECTS OF A RESPONSIVE HEART: PEACE WITH GOD AND FELLOWSHIP WITH OTHERS

READ 2 CHRONICLES 34:26–33.

Huldah: [26]"But to the king of Judah who sent you to Me, I, the Eternal God of Israel, *have noticed your reforms.* [27]Because you recognized the True God's laws, which convicted your nation of their sins, and you humbled yourself and mourned *your nation's actions* by tearing your clothing, I have heard you *and will have mercy on you.* [28]You will die and lie with your ancestors in peace *before I unleash My anger on this nation,* so your eyes will not witness the great disaster that I am about to bring forth on this place and those dwelling here."

The four servants gave the king this message, [29]and he immediately summoned all the elders in Judah and Jerusalem. [30]The entire nation (great and small, priest and layman, man and woman) went up to the Eternal's temple where Josiah read to them the laws from the book of the covenant that was found in the Eternal's temple. [31–32]There, the king and the entire assembly in Jerusalem, people from Benjamin *and Judah,* stood and renewed *Israel's* covenant with the Eternal, promising to follow His ways, obey His laws with all diligence, and perform the duties of the covenant described in the book. Then all the people in Jerusalem respected their covenant with the True God, the God of their ancestors, [33]and Josiah purged all the lands of Israel of false worship, making certain everyone in Israel served the Eternal God. The people remained faithful to the Eternal God of their ancestors throughout Josiah's reign.

PEACE WITH GOD

Ginny: While waiting anxiously at St. Louis Children's Hospital for Shiloh's conclusive diagnosis, Steve's shock gave way to grief. "I cried out to God, 'How could this be? Why her? Why not me? She does not deserve this,'" he recounts poignantly. "As the tears fell I said, 'Lord, I can't do this.' In that moment, I heard God clearly whisper,

'But I can.' An unusual peace washed over me. I realized that a story was being written that was far greater than anything I could comprehend. I was not the story's author, only a part of the story."

The peace of God surrounds Steve and Kristy's lives and Shiloh's story. "My experience with God in that hospital room flashes through my mind often," Steve says. "When I feel like I can't manage what's in front of me, I remember God saying, 'But I can.' That simple reminder keeps me moving forward."

Kristy agrees. "Nearly every day, I read these words from Philippians 4," she recites. "'Don't worry about anything; instead . . . tell God what you need, and thank him for all he has done. Then you will experience God's peace, which exceeds anything we can understand'" (Phil. 4:6–7 NLT). "I simply cannot live without this peace."

Andrew: Peace is a hot topic in our modern-society chatter. The word "peace" itself is rarely uttered except in wartime vernacular, but our search for the right medication, the best sleeping pattern, the most accurate religion all point to the pursuit of a deep breath of contentedness, for some sound mind, for some peace.

Don't get me wrong. I am an avid supporter of being responsible for your own mental and emotional health. We are not victims of our circumstances or culture. But from my own "to hell and back" experiences, and observing others' midnight scenarios, those who regularly own up to their humanness through surrender to God are those with the greatest inner contentment. And so I have discovered that spiritual health is essential to being a person of peace. And people of peace can make wise, often difficult decisions, while still extending grace to themselves and others.

Shiloh Branson, despite her critical circumstances, is alive with peace. Wanting to share that peace to those around her, she recently asked her parents, "What can I do to help everyone know

Jesus? If I can tell them all how good He is, I know they will want Him to be in their hearts." He has brought peace to her very human, fragile heart.

Ginny: Directly following His decree of destruction, God shifts His focus to Josiah and delivers a message of mercy on Judah to honor their king's faithfulness to Him. Josiah's responsive heart has moved God. He has mercy on the king, promising Josiah that in his lifetime Judah will be spared the trauma of judgment previously issued. This leads me to ponder the many times God offers His peace to responsive hearts.

From the beginning of time, God has delivered people from unbelievable circumstances into His peace. He promises peace to the Israelites as He leads them out of Egypt: "I will grant peace in the land, and you will lie down and no one will make you afraid" (Lev. 26:6 NIV). Even in the height of Israel's rebellion, Isaiah promises the Israelites God's perfect peace when they trust in Him (Isa. 26:3) and forecasts the "perfect peace" coming in human form: "And he will be called Wonderful Counselor, Mighty God, Everlasting Father, Prince of Peace" (Isa. 9:6 NIV). Psalm 85:8 says that God "promises peace to his people" (NIV). Jews for Jesus.org describes *shalom*, the Hebrew word for peace, as "completion or wholeness, entering into . . . a restored relationship."[5]

As I encounter God in the Old Testament, I find Him giving His peace to any person with a heart surrendered to Him.

FELLOWSHIP WITH OTHERS

Ginny: When Josiah's confidants relay God's message to him, he reacts as he has in every other situation: by taking action. Instead of breathing a selfish sigh of relief knowing that he will miss Judah's destruction, Josiah gathers all Israelites—Judah and Israel—together at the temple. This is the first time that God's people have been united since the division of the kingdom several hundred years before. And it is the last time they will convene until they shuffle home from Babylonian captivity.

Every Israelite, "great and small, priest and layman, man and woman," listened to Josiah as he read from Scripture, words that none of them had ever heard. Influenced by the open, humble heart of their respected king, the Jewish people unite in their worship of the one true God by renewing their vows to the Eternal and pledging to pursue Him with "all diligence." In other words, with their complete hearts, minds, and souls (2 Chron. 34:29–33).

There is something so attractive about a responsive heart. I have been moved by how Josiah's passion for the Eternal, and his desire for his subjects to possess the same devotion, has resulted in a renewed commitment to God inside the boundaries of his kingdom and beyond. Similarly, I am moved by how Shiloh's heart transplant has affected her love for God and directly impacted her family and community. Through the Bransons' social media pages, folks shared how the experiences of Shiloh and her family have changed their own experiences with God and each other. One person commented, "For me, Shiloh's difficulties were . . . a wake up call to remember what a precious gift life is, and how each day is a blessing from heaven. We will all face hardship in measure. Seeing how Shiloh, and those who love her, have prevailed despite overwhelming difficulty is an assurance that God's grace is sufficient!" Another wrote, "Her journey radically amped up our entire family's faith journey. It brought us closer to each other and to God. And we saw that He is still in the miracle business, as well as the answered prayer business!!"

Countless other responses remind me of how our hearts are moved by experiences that bleed honesty and vulnerability, perhaps because we can all relate. "Because our need has been great, we have learned to pray and trust," Steve shares. "And Shiloh's fearless faith is often the catalyst for our continued prayer and trust."

I aspire to possess faith, unwavering in my pursuit of God, like Josiah and Shiloh, trusting His words and never fearing to ask for His mercies and His miracles. And I want to always reflect His heart as I love Him and serve others.

QUESTIONS for Reflection

1. Why did King Josiah destroy the altars, rather than just making it illegal to worship there? Why did he burn the bones of the priests of Baal on those altars?

2. What do King Josiah's actions reveal about God's view of idolatry?

3. What idols do people have in our modern culture? What things have become idols at times in your own life?

4. How would God have you cleanse your own life of anything that competes with Him for priority in your heart?

5. Why does God promise to "curse this nation and these people" (2 Chron. 34:24)? What had they done to bring this curse upon themselves? What does this suggest about the importance of obedience to God's Word?

6. Is there anything in your own life at present that you need to confess and bring before God?

WITHOUT YOU

(Words and Music: Ginny Owens)

You dance with me the way that we danced long ago
And tenderly breathed life into my dying soul
Never would I have imagined I'd wander so far
So far away
But now as the tears fall
We both speak the words that our hearts have so
  longed to say
I can't live
I can't live
Oh I can't live without You, without You
Anymore
Life for me seemed easy without all the rules
Thought I was free, till freedom declared me the fool
I couldn't hear You whispering to me
Above all of the noise
But now as You hold me, the world fades away
And I'm changed by Your beautiful voice
I'll tell You again how foolish I've been
Though You know more than I can confess
And we dance in Your love, knowing grace is enough
To make this a beautiful mess

© 2005 ChickPower Anthems / ASCAP

EPILOGUE

"The hardness of God is kinder than the softness of
men, and His compulsion is our liberation."

—C. S. Lewis, *Surprised by Joy*[1]

This book was born out of conversation with friends in our
spiritual communities. At first, we were writing this book for
their benefit, for someone else, to awaken the discovery process
for followers of Christ who couldn't find a way to reconcile a New
Testament Redeemer with an Old Testament God. We thought
this book was for them.

But as we delved deeper into the Scriptures, we found more
than we reckoned. Inside the ancient handwriting was much to
learn, to uncover and probe in our own spiritual lives. No, the Old
Testament isn't easy. But it is beautiful.

We extended an open invitation to God of the BC and the
ancient Israelites to infiltrate our twenty-first-century experiences.
We were renewed by the correspondence. Instead of pitting our
minds against some totalitarian godhead that bore little to no
influence on the way we think, process, feel, and imagine today, we
discovered a compassionate Creator on a steady mission to nurture
relationship with humanity—flaws and all. Sounds a bit like love,
doesn't it?

In Matthew 22, in a persnickety plot to entangle Jesus in a catch
twenty-two, the Jewish Pharisees pose Him this question: "Teacher,
of all the laws, which commandment is the greatest?" Jesus, God
incarnate, coolly but pointedly recites Moses' Old Testament tenet:
"'Love the Eternal One your God with all your heart and all your
soul and all your mind.' This is the first and greatest commandment"
(vv. 36–38).

Jesus, always conscious of teaching through relating, plays by their rules and speaks in their terms. Then He points to the bigger picture. He circumvents their petty manipulations and digs deep into core matters. He gets to the heart.

He then takes the intangibles of the first commandment and cements them in practical relationship. "And the second is nearly as important, 'Love your neighbor as yourself'" (v. 39).

Even Jesus knows that loving God needs hands and feet, a little knee-deep action, some nitty-gritty service of worship to exercise the belief that God is for us, all of us, and loves us without condition.

As if anticipating some other attempt by the legalistic tribe to slow Him down with semantics, Jesus issues a final thought to send them on home: "The rest of the law, and all the teachings of the prophets, are but variations on these themes" (v. 40). Everything you have read, studied, researched, staked a claim to die on is dependent on one thing: love.

As we read, studied, researched, and opened our minds to God's unyielding interactions with the Israelites, we recognized His presence in the details, protection from the circumstances, and His concern for the outcome. We discovered a relationship driven by love.

The mystery of the Eternal is well and alive. The more we seek to uncover and understand His character through the Jewish timeline throughout Scripture, the more we are convinced that it is impossible to separate the Old Testament God from the New Testament Messiah, and the more Jesus' creed to love God best by loving each other better echoes through the chambers of Scripture and the hallows of our heart.

God is love. Just ask the Old Testament.

NOTES

PREFACE

1. Madeleine L'Engle, *Walking on Water: Reflections on Faith and Art* (Wheaton, IL: Shaw Publishers, 1980), 62.

CHAPTER 1

1. John Ortberg, *Faith and Doubt* (Grand Rapids, MI: Zondervan, 2008), 121.
2. Brene Brown, *Daring Greatly* (New York: Gotham, 2012).

CHAPTER 2

1. Elisabeth Eliot, *Through Gates of Splendor* (New York: Harper, 1957), 268.
2. Adam Clarke, "Commentary of the Whole Bible," *Sacred Texts*, accessed October 27, 2014, http://www.sacred-texts.com/bib/cmt/clarke/sa1001.htm.
3. Victor Yap, "Prayer Changes People: Sermon Shared by Victor Yap," *SermonCentral*, accessed May 3, 2014, http://www.sermoncentral.com/sermons/prayer-changes-people-victor-yap-sermon-on-samuel-53832.asp?Page=2,.
4. C.S. Lewis, *Mere Christianity* (London: Geoffrey Bles, 1952).
5. Andrew Murray, *With Christ in the School of Prayer* (New York: Fleming H. Revell Company, 1887), 170.

CHAPTER 3

1. Bob Goff, *Love Does* (Nashville, TN: Thomas Nelson, 2012), 137.
2. Dietrich Bonhoeffer, eds. Geffrey B. Kelly and F. Burton Nelson, "Jesus Christ and the Essence of Christianity," *A Testament to Freedom: The Essential Writings of Dietrich Bonhoeffer* (New York: HarperCollins, 1995), 52.
3. C.S. Lewis, *The Lion the Witch and the Wardrobe* (London: Geoffrey Bles, 1950).
4. Jonathan Merritt, "Billy Graham's grandson takes Christians to task: An interview with Tullian Tchividjian," *Religious News Service*, September 23, 2014, http://jonathanmerritt.religionnews.com/2013/10/02/tullian-tchividjian/.

CHAPTER 4

1. Timothy Keller, "Who is the Lord?" (sermon, Redeemer Presbyterian Church, New York, NY, September 22, 2002).
2. John Piper, "I AM Who I AM" (sermon, Bethlehem Baptist Church, Minneapolis, MN, September 16, 1984).
3. Ronald F. Youngblood, gen. ed., *Nelson's Illustrated Bible Dictionary, New and Enhanced Edition* (Nashville: Thomas Nelson, 2014), s.v. "Israel."

CHAPTER 6

1. "Honor," *Google.com*, September 23, 2014, https://www.google.com/?gws_rd=ssl#q=honor.
2. George Ritzer, *Studyguide for Contemporary Sociological Theory and Its Classical Roots: The Basics*, 3rd ed., (Content Technologies, Inc., 2013).
3. "Pluralism, n.," *OED Online*, September 24, 2014, http://dictionary.oed.com/.
4. Charles Garland and Tim Keller, "Pluralism As a Religious Philosophy," *Monergism.com*, September 24, 2014, http://www.monergism.com/thethreshold/articles/onsite/keller.html.
5. Iain W. Provan, *1 and 2 Kings: Understanding the Bible Commentary Series* (Grand Rapids, MI: Baker Publishing Group, 1995), Kindle edition, location 2757.
6. Timothy Keller, "Fire on the Mountain" (sermon, Redeemer Presbyterian Church, New York, NY, September 19, 1999).

CHAPTER 7

1. Antonio Porchia, *Voces*, trans. by W.S. Merwin (Port Townsend, WA: Copper Canyon Press, 2003).
2. William Shakespeare, *Macbeth*, Act IV, scene 3, ll. 209–210.
3. Amy Grant, *Mosaic: Pieces of My Life So Far* (New York: Flying Dolphin Press, 2007), 21–22.
4. "Compassion," *Dictionary*.com, September 24, 2014, http://dictionary.reference.com/browse/compassion?s=t.
5. Suzanne Collins, *The Hunger Games* (New York: Scholastic Press, 2008).

CHAPTER 8

1. Frederick Buechner, *Wishful Thinking: A Theological ABC* (New York: Harper and Row, 1973).
2. Kim Lawton, "Frederick Buechner Extended Interview," *Religion & Ethics Newsweekly*, September 23, 2014, http://www.pbs.org/wnet/religionandethics/2003/04/18/april-18-2003-frederick-buechner-extended-interview/8658/.
3. "Holiness," *Biblestudytools.org*, September 23, 2014, http://www.biblestudytools.com/dictionary/holiness/.
4. Philip Yancey, *What's So Amazing About Grace*, (Grand Rapids, MI: Zondervan, 1997), 190.
5. http://www.jewsforjesus.org/publications/newsletter/december-1997/studyonbiblical

EPILOGUE

1. C. S. Lewis, *Surprised by Joy: The Shape of My Early Life* (London: Geoffrey Bles, 1955), 198.

ABOUT THE AUTHORS

ANDREW GREER is a #1-selling singer/songwriter and co-creator of the innovative "Hymns for Hunger" Tour with Dove Award-winning singer/songwriter Cindy Morgan, utilizing music to help raise awareness and resources for hunger relief organizations in communities across the nation. A 2013 GMA Dove Award nominee, Greer's *All Things Bright & Beautiful: Hymns for the Seasons* held the #1 spot on Nielsen Christian SoundScan's Instrumental chart for 25 weeks. That same year, *Angel Band: The Christmas Sessions* landed in the Top 10 on iTunes' Singer/Songwriter chart, while its 2012 predecessor *Angel Band: The Hymn Sessions* reached #2 on Amazon's Contemporary Folk chart. Greer has collaborated with some of the top names in bluegrass and Gospel music, including Sandi Patty, Sonya Isaacs, The McCrary Sisters, Phil Madeira, and Ron Block of Alison Krauss & Union Station. Also a respected writer, Andrew's writings have appeared in publications like *Christianity Today*, *In Touch* and *Parenting Teens* magazine. He lives in Franklin, Tennessee.

GINNY OWENS, a three-time Dove Award winner, became a household name when she was named Gospel Music Association's "New Artist of the Year" in 2000. In a career that has spanned fifteen years, Ginny's eight studio recordings have amassed nearly one million records in sales and spawned career-defining number ones like "If You Want Me To" and "Free." Her songwriting prowess has earned her song cuts by artist peers like Rachael Lampa and Christian music legend Michael W. Smith, and awarded Ginny a mantle of ASCAP and BMG Music Publishing Awards.

Born and raised in Jackson, Mississippi, Owens discovered melodies on the piano before she could complete a sentence. As her vision began to leave her eyes—a degenerative eye condition left Ginny completely blind by age three—songs began to emerge from her fingertips, providing a window into the world for Owens. Despite her physical challenge, the illustrious songstress pursued a career in music. Her unique musical style and inspirational lyrics have transcended genre definition, endearing her to Christian and mainstream listeners alike to afford her audiences at the White House, the Sundance Film Festival, Lilith Fair and a rare performance at the 60th annual National Day of Prayer in Washington, D.C.

When not on the road, the Tennessee resident serves as an adjunct professor of songwriting at her Nashville alma mater, Belmont University, and is on staff as a worship leader at The People's Church in Franklin, Tennessee. In 2005, Owens launched The Fingerprint Initiative, a hands-on nonprofit organization designed to "bring hope to the world, one touch at a time."

REFRACTION

GOD ALIGNS PEOPLE OF FAITH TO HIS PURPOSES

Thomas Nelson's Refraction collection of books offers biblical responses to the biggest issues of our time, topics that have been tabooed or ignored in the past. The books will give readers insights into these issues and what God says about them, and how to respond to others whose beliefs differ from ours in a transparent and respectful way. Refraction books cross theological boundaries in an open and honest way, through succinct and candid writing for a contemporary, millenial-minded reader.

LEARN MORE AT REFRACTIONBOOKS.COM

NOW AVAILABLE   NOW AVAILABLE   NOW AVAILABLE   APRIL 2015   JULY 2015